First Print Edition [1.0] -1433 h. (2012 c.e.)

Copyright © 1433 H./2012 C.E.
Taalib al-Ilm Educational Resources

http://taalib.com
Learn Islaam, Live Islaam.^{SM}

I0158735

ISBN EAN-13: 978-1-938117-41-1   [Soft cover Print Edition]

GOLDEN WORDS UPON GOLDEN WORDS...
FOR EVERY MUSLIM.

"Imaam al-Barbahaaree, may Allaah have mercy upon him said:

May Allaah have mercy upon you! Examine carefully the speech of everyone you hear from in your time particularly. So do not act in haste and do not enter into anything from it until you ask and see: Did any of the Companions of the Prophet, may Allaah's praise and salutations be upon him, speak about it, or did any of the scholars? So if you find a narration from them about it, cling to it, do not go beyond it for anything and do not give precedence to anything over it and thus fall into the Fire.

Explanation by Sheikh Saaleh al-Fauzaan, may Allaah preserve him:

'Do not be hasty in accepting as correct what you may hear from the people especially in these later times. As now there are many who speak about so many various matters, issuing rulings and ascribing to themselves both knowledge and the right to speak. This is especially the case after the emergence and spread of new modern day media technologies. Such that everyone now can speak and bring forth that which is in truth worthless; by this meaning words of no true value - speaking about whatever they wish in the name of knowledge and in the name of the religion of Islaam. It has even reached the point that you find the people of misguidance and the members of the various groups of misguidance and deviance from the religion speaking as well. Such individuals have now become those who speak in the name of the religion of Islaam through means such as the various satellite television channels. Therefore be very cautious!

It is upon you oh Muslim, and upon you oh student of knowledge individually, to verify matters and not rush to embrace everything and anything you may hear. It is upon you to verify the truth of what you hear, asking, 'Who else also makes this same statement or claim?', 'Where did this thought or concept originate or come from?', 'Who is its reference or source authority?'. Asking what are the evidences which support it from within the Book and the Sunnah? And inquiring where has the individual who is putting this forth studied and taken his knowledge from? From who has he studied the knowledge of Islaam?

Each of these matters requires verification through inquiry and investigation, especially in the present age and time. As it is not every speaker who should rightly be considered a source of knowledge, even if he is well spoken and eloquent, and can manipulate words captivating his listeners. Do not be taken in and accept him until you are aware of the degree and scope of what he possesses of knowledge and understanding. As perhaps someone's words may be few, but possess true understanding, and perhaps another will have a great deal of speech yet he is actually ignorant to such a degree that he doesn't actually posses anything of true understanding. Rather he only has the ability to enchant with his speech so that the people are deceived. Yet he puts forth the perception that he is a scholar, that he is someone of true understanding and comprehension, that he is a capable thinker, and so forth. Through such means and ways he is able to deceive and beguile the people, taking them away from the way of truth.

Therefore what is to be given true consideration is not the amount of the speech put forth or that one can extensively discuss a subject. Rather the criterion that is to be given consideration is what that speech contains within it of sound authentic knowledge, what it contains of the established and transmitted principles of Islaam. As perhaps a short or brief statement which is connected to or has a foundation in the established principles can be of greater benefit than a great deal of speech which simply rambles on, and through hearing you don't actually receive very much benefit from.

This is the reality which is present in our time; one sees a tremendous amount of speech which only possesses within it a small amount of actual knowledge. We see the presence of many speakers yet few people of true understanding and comprehension.' "

[The eminent major scholar Sheikh Saaleh al-Fauzaan, may Allaah preserve him- 'A Valued Gift for the Reader Of Comments Upon the Book Sharh as-Sunnah', page 102-103]

STATEMENTS FROM THE SCHOLARS REGARDING CLARIFYING THE CALLERS TO THE TRUTH FROM THE CALLERS TO FALSEHOOD

Translated & Compiled By
Abu Sukhailah Khalil Ibn-Abelahyi al-Amreekee

Table of Contents

بسم الله الرحمن الرحيم

Compilers Introduction

Verily, all praise is due to Allaah, we praise Him, we seek His assistance and we ask for His forgiveness. We seek refuge in Him from the evils of our souls and the evils of our actions. Whoever Allaah guides, no one can lead him astray and whoever is caused to go astray, there is no one that can guide him. I bear witness that there is no deity worthy of worship except Allaah alone with no partners. And I bear witness that Muhammad is His worshipper and Messenger, peace and salutations be upon him, his household, his Companions, and all those who follow his guidance until the day of Judgment. To proceed:

Any Muslim who takes the time to look carefully around him at the Muslims in our age will fully understand the statement of the noble scholar, Sheikh Muhammad 'Umar Bazmool:

"A Muslim in our present age sees tremendous differing all around him among the Muslims, no matter in what direction he turns! Whether this is in the area of properly understanding the source texts of Islaam in different rulings in matters of ritual worship or in everyday dealings, or in relation to the correct methodology of calling the people to the religion, or any other issue!

Such that among the Muslims there are those who just stand bewildered and confused in the face of all this differing. As upon every separate way there are those calling and inviting to it- making it attractive, legitimizing and justifying their way, yet disguising what they have of falsehood by holding up in front of it an element of the truth, such that it is almost impossible for the general people to distinguish what is correct!" [1]

---

[1]   Islaam Alaa Muftariq at-Turuq of Sheikh Muhammad Bazmool page 1.

This pocket edition, which is the first publication of our new series *"Standing up for the Sunnah"*, is a collection of selected articles which were appendixes from one of our other publications, *"A Lighthouse of Knowledge from a Guardian of the Sunnah...."*. They have been gathered together with additional scholarly texts and answered questions regarding the essential subject of the importance of clarifying and defending the religion of Islaam by distinguishing what actually is part of Islaam and what is not.

The Muslim today is faced with many movements and groups from among themselves which are claiming to call to and raise the banner of making Islaam a reality. Sheikh Muhammad Ibn Ibraaheem, may Allaah have mercy upon him, who was the principal jurist issuing the overall religious rulings for the entire kingdom of Saudi Arabia earlier in this century, stated:

"Indeed, many of the people attribute themselves to Islaam, stating the two declarations of faith, performing the outward pillars of Islaam; yet this solely is not sufficient to correctly judge their ascription to Islaam, nor does it legitimize the practices they have engrossed themselves in of associating others with Allaah in acts of worship such as supplication to and seeking assistance from the prophets of Allaah and the righteous from among His deceased worshippers, as well as other practices which cause one to leave Islaam.

And this practice of distinguishing and differentiating between the many who all claim or attribute themselves to Islaam, is a matter well established in the evidences of the Book of Allaah and the Sunnah, as well as the consensus of the first generations of this Ummah and its leading people of knowledge." [2]

---

[2]   'Aqeedah al-Muwahhideen, page 392

These selections are intended to clarify some of the many misconceptions in this area that are found among today's Muslims through evidence-based scholastic discussions of different ideas and concepts. Discussions which for that sincere Muslim whom Allaah has mercy upon, and who is willing to consider and weigh the evidences and proofs related to this issue, will affect and reach his heart, leading to the affirmation and acknowledgement that this responsibility, carried out by the people of knowledge, has, and will always be, part of Islaam. These different articles from various eminent scholars discuss the evidences and principles of this subject which are at very heart of what is needed to address the confusion seen among Muslims as mentioned by Sheikh Bazmool, by returning the discussion among other things, back to defining the essential nature of Islaam itself as its Prophet defined it, and constant need to preserve it from changes and alterations.

Connected to this, as an indispensable aspect of clarification, is the indication of who- meaning which individuals- are calling to that perfect complete religion which our Prophet called to, and who is calling to one of the many changed, adapted, remodeled, allegedly "improved" versions of Islaam. Yet one of the first hurdles many Muslims encounter is the misconception quickly put forth that mistakes of others should not be discussed. Furthermore it is often falsely claimed that considering and identifying people as part of that specific movement, organization, way or "understanding" of Islaam, they openly hold, call to, and practice, even in a scholarly manner, is wrong and impermissible!

Alhamdulillah, the falsehood of this claim is clarified comprehensively from many of its angles within the first evidence based article of the compilation which is by Sheikh 'Abdus-Salaam Ibn Burjis, may Allaah have mercy upon him.

How many have been deceived into turning away from this essential practice of seeking from the scholars clarifying statements about claims and those who made those claims through the false statement: "Look at what they do, calling names, using labels and labeling! We are all Muslims! We must abandon this!".

Sheikh Burjis, may Allaah have mercy upon him, effectively indicates that this practice of clarification takes its basis from the Sunnah, that this practice is essential to the preservation of the religion as found within the statements of our scholars, and that it was undoubtedly practiced by the first generations of Muslims as well as all those who followed them through the centuries of history of this Muslim Ummah. The renowned scholar Ibn Taymeeyah, may Allaah have mercy upon him, stated,

".. The clarification of the misguided state of those who innovate and warning the Muslim Ummah from them is an obligation by consensus of all the Muslims, such that it was said to Ahmad Ibn Hanbal, "Is the man who fasts, prays the ritual prayer, and spends time in seclusion for worship more beloved to you, or the one who speaks about the errors of those who have innovated in the religion?" He replied, "If someone stands in prayers or secludes himself for ritual worship, then certainly this is for his own sake, but when someone speaks regarding the errors of the people of innovation, then certainly this is for the sake of all of the Muslims, and this is greater in value."

This makes clear that benefiting the general Muslims in their knowledge of the religion is from among the types of jihaad in the path of Allaah, for the sake of His religion, His legislated ways, and His Sharee'ah. The defending against the harms of these innovators and opposing them for this reasons is a collective obligation which all the Muslims have agreed upon. If Allaah did not bring forth those who stand up to defend the people from the harm coming from these innovators, the religion would become corrupted; and this type of corruption is more severe than the occupation of Muslim lands by enemies from among the people at war with the Muslims. As those foreign occupiers when they seize and take over a land do not corrupt the hearts and what they, meaning those occupied Muslim peoples, hold to be this religion except for those who embrace them, but as for these innovators then they corrupt the hearts of the Muslims from the very beginning." [3]

However this first misunderstanding, meaning blatant rejection of clarifying refutations and the scholars classifying individuals who call to innovations in the religion, is one which is often interwoven with other supporting and similar misconceptions which also lack any detailed support within the source texts of Islaam, the consensus of the scholars of the Muslim Ummah, or the statements of the leading scholars throughout the centuries. The defense of many of these supporting false ideas and newly developed principles is, along with other matters, often based upon:

1. an incorrect explanation of certain general evidences while neglecting others specific textual evidences
2. deceptive selective arguments which have the appearance of correctness
3. correct assertions which are used or applied incorrectly.
4. emotional arguments without scholastic support

As such, the other articles in the compilation directly address many of these incorrect ideas and principles in a very clear definitive manner.

---

[3] Majmu'a al-Fataawaa: vol.28, page 231

The remaining articles also present to the reader some of the evidences and discussions of this subject from the direction of the practice of Messenger of Allaah himself, may the praise and salutations of Allaah be upon him, from the best generations who most properly understood and practiced his guidance, as well as from that which is known from all those guided Muslims who followed them throughout history including our present century.

These clarifications help us understand how the practice of refutation of mistakes is properly implemented and by whom, giving insight into what is the proper balance reflected by the leading scholars which avoids both extremism and negligence. As the statements of these scholars indicating the legitimacy and fundamental importance of this practice is not a call for those who are not from the people of knowledge to enter into an area which is not their domain- as is mentioned by Sheikh Burjis, may Allaah have mercy upon him. But is a evidenced general and specific affirmation of the role of evidenced clarifications in preserving the religion of Islaam throughout the centuries.

This compilation closes with a brief summary of eight points which I pray will help the reader understand the issue and matter comprehensively as an essential part of this noble preserved religion.

May the praise and salutations of Allaah be upon the Messenger of Allaah, his household, his Companions, and all those who followed his guidance until the Day of Judgement. And all praise is due to Allaah alone, Lord of all the worlds.

Written by Abu Sukhailah
Khalil Ibn-Abelahyi al-Amreekee
1st of Muharram, 1434

(1)

A SCHOLAR'S KNOWLEDGE BASED REBUTTAL
OF THOSE WHO REJECT OF THE PRACTICE OF
CATEGORIZING PEOPLE ACCORDING TO
THE BELIEFS AND PATH THEY
CALL TO & STAND UPON
BY SHEIKH 'ABDUS-SALAAM IBN BURJIS,
MAY ALLAAH HAVE MERCY UPON HIM

In the name of Allaah, the Most Gracious, the Most Merciful

All praise is due to Allaah, we praise Him, we seek His assistance and we ask for His forgiveness, and we repent to Him. We seek refuge in Him from the evils of our souls and the evils of our actions. Whoever Allaah guides, no one can lead him astray and whoever is caused to go astray, there is no one that can guide him. I bear witness that there is none worthy of worship except Allaah alone having no partners. And I bear witness that Muhammad is His worshipper and Messenger.

❈Oh you who believe, fear Allaah as He ought to be feared and do not die except while you are Muslims. ❈–(Surah al-Imraan: 102)

.*❈Oh mankind, fear Allaah who created you from a single soul and from that, He created its mate. And from them He brought forth many men and women. And fear Allaah to whom you demand your mutual rights. Verily, Allaah is an ever All-Watcher over you ❈*–(Surah an-Nisaa: 1)

❈ Oh you who believe, fear Allaah and speak a word that is truthful (and to the point) - He will rectify your deeds and forgive you your sins. And whoever obeys Allaah and His Messenger has achieved a great success.❈–(Surah al-Ahzaab: 70-71)

As for what follows:

Indeed, the fact that Allaah the Most Perfect and the Most High, has blessed one who is Muslim, one who worships Him, with success in acting in conformance to the guidance of the pure Sunnah and success to proceed upon its straight path is indeed a tremendous blessing and bounty, my brothers, which requires thankfulness and abundant remembrance of Allaah. As adherence to the Sunnah today is something rare, with the one who holds firmly to seen as strange. In truth, the strangeness of adherence to the Sunnah is one aspect of the general emergence of state of strangeness of those standing upon truth, which we were informed by the Prophet, may Allaah's praise and salutations be upon him, would occur. As today the majority of societies do not adhere to the guidance of the Sunnah, the situation is just as was once stated by Imaam Sufyaan at-Thawree, may Allaah have mercy upon him:

"Desire good for the people of the Sunnah, as indeed they are strangers among the people." Or as was stated by Abu Bakr Ibn 'Ayaash, may Allaah the Most High have mercy upon him, *"True adherence to the Sunnah within the practice of Islaam, is something treasured just as the distinction and eminence of path of Islaam among the other religions."* And Yunus Ibn 'Ubayd, may Allaah the Most High have mercy upon him, *"There is nothing rarer than the true Sunnah, except the rarity of the one who truly understands and comprehends it."*

So my brothers, if such were the statements of those leading scholars in that early age they lived in, so how much more do they apply to our situation in this later age of ours? There is no doubt that the strangeness of the authentic practice of the Sunnah has only increased in the intensity of its rareness and strangeness among the people, and therefore so has its importance and significance. Certainly there is no strength nor power to change from one state to another except through Allaah, the Exalted, the Mighty. For that reason the one who is from the people of the Sunnah, he should praise Allaah the Most high for the blessing of this bounty, and ask Allaah the Most Perfect and the Most High to make him firm upon that blessing.

As for the one who is not from among those people upon the Sunnah, how evil is his state, how significant is the trial he has fallen into, and how pitiful is his condition! He must turn back to his Lord the Most Perfect and the Most High, and return back to the true practice of his religion. As Islaam is the Sunnah and the Sunnah is Islaam, one will not be established without the other. From the tremendous blessing of Allaah the Most Perfect and the Most High upon humanity is that He the Most Exalted, the Most Magnificent has not allowed that they be any age from the passing ages of human life, after the age of His final messenger, except that some of the people of the Sunnah are found within it, establishing the proofs of Allaah upon all of the people. They convey and spread the revealed Sharee'ah of Allaah the Most Perfect and the Most High just as it was brought by the Messenger of Allaah, may Allaah's praise and salutations be upon him.

They invite the people to adhere to the Sunnah, and to turn away from both innovated matters in the religion as well as the following of their desires. And certainly we have become familiar with the fact that the people of the Sunnah and the Jama'ah, from everything that has been transmitted to us of information concerning their state of affairs, various circumstances, their life and societal histories; that they indeed gathered upon the Sunnah despite the distance between their various countries, and the separation between their different lands, while having mutual feelings of connection between themselves, and loving one another. Even if they never actually saw each other, just as Sufyaan ath-Thawree, may Allaah the Most High have mercy upon him, said:

"If it reaches you that there is a man in the east of the earth who is someone upon the Sunnah and there is another in the west of the earth who also stands upon the Sunnah, then send your greeting of salaam to them and pray for both of them. As how few are the people of the Sunnah and the Jama'ah!" Likewise Ayyub as-Sakhtiyaanee, may Allaah the Most High have mercy upon him, said, *"Indeed, when I am informed of the death of someone from the people of the Sunnah then it is as if someone has severed one of my limbs from my body."*

Yet today, how many people attribute themselves to the Sunnah, and how numerous are there who have dressed themselves in the outward show and appearance of the people of the Sunnah, such that distinguishing between those who are truly the people of the Sunnah from those who are not- is not at all an easy or simple matter. And those individuals who deceptively present the outward appearance of the people of the Sunnah, and outwardly show adherence to it -do not do so except in an attempt to eventually ruin and devastate the unity of the people of the Sunnah and the Jama'ah, striving to bring division into their ranks, and to turn some of them against others among them.

All in order that eventually they will be able to raise up the flag of their innovation in the religion, and swell the numbers of those standing in their ranks. Nonetheless they plot and plan, and Allaah also plans, yet certainly Allaah is the best of planners. As in regard to the situation of the people of the Sunnah, when such people of this evil aim struggle to infiltrate among them, dressing themselves in the garments of the Sunnah to enable their plotting, then it is seen that Allaah tears the curtain away from the hidden reality of this infiltrator and exposes him. As no one attempts to hide such an evil aim, except that Allaah the Most Perfect and the Most High uncovers it and brings it out through the slips of his tongue or the unguarded expressions of his face which reflects their orientation.

The significant danger of this situation which I have indicated is that in our age many people have falsely dressed themselves in the garments of adherence to the Sunnah, when in reality they are not people of the Sunnah. The severity of the spread of this practice, causes my fear of the near extinguishing of path and way of the people of the Sunnah and the Jama'ah at the hands of these people who falsely designate themselves with this name but in fact do not deserve in any way to carry it .

Therefore in this sitting we will discuss some of the issues, and some of the matters or affairs that are being put forward in this age in the name of the people of the Sunnah and the Jama'ah. And these affairs or issues which are being put forward, most of them in general, have no basis in actual knowledge, nor within the way of the righteous predecessors of the first three generations, may Allaah the Most High have mercy upon them. Rather they are fabrications attributed to their true way and methodology as a fraud and deception, either being put forward in order to give victory to a specific party or organization from those various groups which have spread in this age in the name of Islaam, or simply in accordance to someone's desires, or something similar to this from these distressing matters.

So I say, that when these matters are being put forth, such as the various matters being falsely presented in the name of the people of the Sunnah and the Jama'ah, while in reality they are far from deserving this name, then it becomes obligatory for an individual to warn against this to the degree that he finds himself able to. As such we in this brief sitting, will try to mention some of these matters. And we hope to establish and indicate what is correct through this by that guidance which Allaah the Most Perfect and the Most High, guides us with in this; hoping that He grants both us and you sincerity in seeking His pleasure alone, the blessing of truly adhering to and following the Messenger of Allaah, may Allaah's praise and salutations be upon him, as well as guidance to truly proceed upon the path and way of the righteous predecessors of the first three generations, may Allaah be pleased with them.

From these issues is the issue of categorizing the people according to their belief and way, the issue of ruling by other than that which Allaah revealed, the issue of whether disbelief occurs only through denial of the legitimacy of that matter in Islaam, or by this joined / along with other factors, as well as the issue of the legitimacy of multiple groups, parties, and organizations, and having biased divisive partisanship toward one of them. So we will start with the issue of categorizing the people according to their belief and way. Is this practice valid in the Sharee'ah or incorrect, and is categorizing people by using conjecture correct or not?

THE FOUNDATION OF THE PRACTICE OF CATEGORIZING PEOPLE IS FROM THE PROPHET

In response to that question, it should be stated that the practice of categorization which is correct is the attribution of an individual who is involved in innovation in the religion to that innovation he is involved in, or what is similar to this. This is comparable to attributing the liar to the practice of lying. This is the case with every related issue of this subject, it is clearly connected to the area of knowledge know as criticism and commendation in the religion.

We say that this categorization of people is the way of truth, and a practice of the religion by which we worship Allaah. Due to this the people of the Sunnah all agree on the practice of attributing to the one whom you know is involved in some form of innovation, to that innovation. Such that the one who in engaged in the innovations related to the denial of qadr or Allaah's decree, then it should be said that he is a "Qadree", and the one who is engaged in the innovations of the sect of the Khawaarij, then it should be said that he is "Khaarijee", and the one who is engaged in the innovations of the innovation of irja', then it should be said that he is "Murji'ee' ", and the one who is engaged in the innovations of the innovation of rafdh, then it should be said that he is "Raafidhee", and the one who is engaged in the innovations of the innovation of the sect of the Ash'areeyah, then it should be said that he is "Asha'ree'", and similarly stating this with the one who is in fact "Mu'tazilee", "Sufee" or so on as necessary.

The foundation of this practice is that the Prophet, may Allaah's praise and salutations be upon him, informed us that his Ummah would divide into seventy three sects, one of which would be successful and saved and the remaining seventy two of which would be punished in the Hellfire. This narration indicates explicitly that there would be many different sects, and it is not possible to conceive of their being different sects without them each having their own separate beliefs and way that the people follow. Therefore if this is the case, then every individual who follows the beliefs and ways of any one of these sects should be directly attributed and connected to his sect.

And the Prophet, may Allaah's praise and salutations be upon him, has mentioned an example from among these sects, that being the Qadareeyah, in his statement, { *The Qadareeyah are the Majoos from this Ummah, when they are sick do not visit them, and when they die then do not pray over them.* } [1] So in relation to the sect of the Qadareeyah, the one who is from them is known as "Qadaree". So the Prophet, may Allaah's praise and salutations be upon him, specifically attributed to individuals from his Ummah that they would come after him an innovated and false belief regarding Qadar, or Allaah's decree. Thus he categorized them according to the innovation they would engaged in, that being the denial of Allaah's qadar or decree. An additional example from one of these sects which also comes directly from the words of the Messenger of Allaah, may Allaah's praise and salutations be upon him, is regarding the sect of the Khawaarij, an individual from them is called a "Khaarijee".

---

[1]   Sheikh al-Albaanee has declared it authentic: Saheeh Sunan Abu Dawud: 4092; Saheeh al-Jaamee'a: 444; as-Sunnah of Ibn Abee 'Aseem: 268

The Prophet, may Allaah's praise and salutations be upon him, discussed this specific sect in so many hadeeth narrations that it reached the high level of ranking of being considered consecutively transmitted or as is stated in hadeeth terminology- mutawaatir. Yet he, may Allaah's praise and salutations be upon him, did not give them the name Khawaarij, it was the Companions who designated this sect with this name. Indeed, there are many narrations which have been transmitted about and regarding the sect of the Khawaarij, while they appeared after the time of the Prophet, may Allaah's praise and salutations be upon him, From these many narrations found in the Musnad and Sunan collections books is the statement of the Prophet, may Allaah's praise and salutations be upon him, in which he said: *{The will come forth in my Ummah differing and separation. And there will be a people who are excellent in speech but evil in their actions, they will recite the Qur'aan but it will not pass beyond their throats. One of you will consider his own salat and fasting meager or slight in comparison to the salat and fasting that they perform, yet they will leave this religion just as the arrow leaves the bow. Then they will never return to it, just as the arrow can never return backwards to the bow. They are the most evil of creation and of created beings. The reward for the one who fights against them or who is killed by them in a battle is Toobah. They claim to call to the Book of Allaah, yet they have no share of the guidance within it. Those who fight against them surely do a service for Allaah regarding them.}* The Messenger of Allaah was asked: what are their characteristics" He said: *{They shave their heads.}* This is an authentic hadeeth narrated by Imaam Ahmad in His Musnad, and Imaam Lalikaaee, and in others collections. Also Imaam Muslim and others relate the narration of Basheer 'Ibn Amr who said, *{I asked Sahl Ibn Haneef, "Did you hear Messenger of Allaah, may Allaah's praise and salutations be upon him, mention the Khawaarij. So he said, "I heard him say, -and he pointed with his hand towards the east- that there will be a* *people who would recite the Qur'aan with their tongues yet it would not go beyond their throat. They will leave this religion just as the arrow leaves the bow.}* This hadeeth is found in Saheeh Muslim, Saheeh al-Bukhaaree, and in the Musnad of Imaam Ahmad.

And further expanding on what has been transmitted about subject of the Khawaarij are the statements of the scholars of the first generations, and their own actions which are clear. They affirmed the reality of this sect and attributed them to those specific innovations which they engaged in by name - as obligated upon them by the Book of Allaah and the Sunnah. And anyone who was known to engage in the innovations of this sect was openly attributed to it by name. All of this is affirmatively transmitted from them and recorded in reliable works in which the Sunnah is preserved, which are not hidden from the people of knowledge. And if an individual was to compile and gather a work the size of a large single volume, it would only encompass part of what is affirmed from them regarding this practice.

Similarly, the books of biography, and life histories, and those authored compilation described as works of the "Sunnah" contain many reports in relation to this subject. These reports are not restricted to what is narrated for example in Saheeh Muslim on the authority of Yahya Ibn Ya'mur that the first man who discussed the issue of Qadar or Allaah's decree in Basra was Ma'bad al-Juhani. Within this narration it states that they met Ibn 'Umar on Hajj and they said to him, "...*There have appeared some people in our land who recite the Holy Qur'aan and pursue knowledge.*" And then after talking about these affairs, they added: "*From what they are upon is that they claim that there is no such thing as divine decree and events are not prewritten.*" He 'Abdullah ibn Umar replied to him saying, *{When you happen to meet such people tell them that I am free from them and they are free from me...}*

23

So they, of the early generation, indicated that there was a people among them who sought to worship Allaah through this issue of qadar, meaning seeking to worship Allaah through the denial of qadar or decree. Therefore they attributed to them the name "al-Qadareeyah". It is reported that Abu Amaamah, may Allah be pleased with him, explained the meaning of the statement of Allaah the Most Perfect and the Most High, ◈*Of those who split up their religion and became sects*◈-(Surah Ar-Rum: 32) he explained it to mean and refer to the sect of the Khawaarij. Also it is reported on the authority of Abu Hurairah, may Allah be pleased with him, that he narrated several similar hadeeths coming from the Prophet, may Allaah's praise and salutations be upon him. However, none of these are affirmed to be authentic. But it is reported that Abu Amaamah, may Allah be pleased with him, additionally explained the meaning of the statement of Allaah the Most Perfect and the Most High, ◈ *And be not as those who divided and differed among themselves after the clear proofs had come to them.* ◈-(Surah Al-Imran: 105) that this means the sect of the Khawaarij.

THE PRACTICE OF CATEGORIZING PEOPLE AMONG THE FIRST GENERATIONS OF MUSLIMS

Furthermore the first generations, may Allaah be pleased with them, generally attributed those who were involved in these innovations and similar ones to that specific innovation. Naafa' Ibn al-'Azraaq was one of the leaders of the Khawaarij, as is well known, and indeed the first generations clearly attributed him by name to this innovated way he was known to be upon. Moreover, at one time his name came to be known among them as a symbol of the sect of the Khawaarij. Such that there came to be was a group from the Khawaarij who were specifically called the "Azaariqah". It is affirmed in 'al-Musnad' of Imaam Ahmad from 'Abdullah Ibn Abee 'Awfah, may Allah be pleased with him, that he said, "*May Allaah's curse be upon the Azaariqah, may Allaah curse be upon the Azaariqah. The Messenger of Allaah, may Allaah's praise and salutations be upon him, informed us that they would be the dogs of the Hellfire.*" The narrator who narrated from him said to him, "*Are the Azaariqah one person from among them or all of them?*" 'Abdullah Ibn Abee 'Awfah replied, "*Rather, they are all those from the sect of the Khawaarij.*"

The "Azaariqah" were fought against during the period of the struggle of 'Abdullah Ibn az-Zubair, may Allaah, the Blessed and the Most High, be pleased with him. And the heads and leaders of the Khawaarij who killed 'Alee Ibn Abee Taalib were well known to the first generations, and the Salaf attributed them by name to this innovation that they were upon. These were such as their leaders 'Abdullah Ibn Wahb, Harqoos Ibn Zaheer, Shareeh Ibn Abee 'Awfah, 'Abdullah Ibn Sakhbarah as-Sulamee, and others.

For example consider this chain of dishonor of innovation and this stain of misguidance: al-Jahm Ibn Safwaan from al-Ja'd Ibn Dirham from Abaan Ibn Sama'aan from Taaloot Ibn al-Aa'asm al-Yahoodee; indeed the people of the Sunnah recognize the wickedness of this chain and warn against these misguided people within it and they attribute everyone whom they know to be connected to this sect to those astray people they walk with, accompany, and are associated with- meaning al-Jahm Ibn Safwaan. Such that they would label someone from those people as a "Jahmee". Similarly with the condition of Ma'bad al-Jahmee and Ghayalaan ad-Dimashqee those who spoke with the innovation of denying Allaah 's decree, and Waasil Ibn 'Ataa' and 'Amr Ibn 'Ubayd from the people of the innovation of the sect of the Mu'tazilah. All these individuals as well as many others besides them were categorized by the Muslims of the first generations, may Allah be pleased with them, and they were then thereafter referred to by names which attributed them to that specific innovation they were upon- without anyone of the people of understanding in that time and age denying this or blaming them.

Additionally if you approach this issue and practice from another direction, we also find that the books which specialize in listing the statements of recommendation and criticism of those transmitting knowledge of this religion are filled with the specific attributions and ascription of various narrators who came in a later time than the period of these specific leaders of misguidance, back to the specific sects and groups that they held the beliefs of. And we have never ceased sharing the methodology, path, and perspective, of the leading scholars who made these statements in such books, in affirming this practice of attributing a person to that which it is confirmed he engaged in and stood upon or similarly the affirmation of any lack of confirmed reports of such and attribution to a specific sect or belief (make simpler).

What is intended by this is making it unambiguous and clear that the people of the Sunnah have always engaged in this categorization, if the reports attributing someone are affirmed and accepted, that the attribution within it is accepted, and if they are not affirmed or rejected then they declared the individual concerned free from that which has been falsely attributed from him.

And I state this specifically because some of what may have been attributed to a specific individual may not be authentic, such that it is not correct to attribute him to that mentioned innovation. This is like the case of what has been mentioned about al-Jawzajaanee Ibraaheem Ibn Yaqoob. Ibn Hibaan stated about him, *"He was Hareezee in his path"* meaning that he allegedly, but incorrectly, accused him of holding the views of Hareez Ibn 'Uthmaan who was someone accused of the innovation of Nasb or hatred for the household of the

Messenger of Allaah, may Allaah's praise and salutations be upon him.

There are comparable examples of their practice of categorizing people found in the statement of Ibn 'Uyainah, may Allaah the Most High have mercy upon him, where he said regarding Ismaa'eel Ibn Samee'a, "He is Bayhasee", or the statement of Ibn Qahtaan about him *"He was Safree and Bayhasee"* attributing him additionally to one of the leaders of the Khawaarij, to whom the scholars attribute a certain group from among them to him specifically. And the Baheeteeyah were a sect from within the Safreeah who followed the way of Zeyaad Ibn al-Asfaar from among the Khawaarij. Similarly Imaam Ahmad, may Allaah the Most High have mercy upon him, said about Sayf Ibn Sulayman, *"He is Qadaree"* and similar descriptions. Statements such as these are found to be plentiful in the books from the scholars of the first three generations, may Allaah the Most High have mercy upon them.

THE LEGITIMACY OF DESCRIPTIVE TERMS USED FOR THE PEOPLE OF THE SUNNAH

Therefore it is affirmed through everything we have just related that the practice of categorizing people is sound and correct, and a practice that the entire Ummah has collectively acknowledged. No one of intelligence denies the legitimacy of this practice. As the people of innovation in the religion are connected and attributed to their specific innovation in order that the people recognize them and are warned against them, likewise the people upon the truth are attributed to the truth and not to anything else. As such they do not have any other titles that would indicate that they have left what is required or demanded by the Book of Allaah and the Sunnah and what the first generation of the Ummah proceeded upon.

This is the meaning of the statement of Imaam Maalik, may Allaah the Most High have mercy upon him,

"*The people of the Sunnah do not have any other titles which they are solely identified as, not as "Jahmee" nor "Qadree", nor "Rafidhee"*". It was mentioned in the work of Ibn 'Abdul-Bar, 'al-Intiqaa", that Imaam Maalik, may Allaah the Most High have mercy upon him, was asked about the Sunnah he replied, "It is that which has no name other than the Sunnah, and he recited the statement of Allaah the Most Perfect and the Most High, ❀ *And verily, this is my Straight Path, so follow it, and follow not other paths, for they will separate you away from His Path.* ❀–(Surah Al-An'am: 153)

Ibn Qayyim, may Allaah the Most High have mercy upon him, mentioned in his work 'Madaarij as-Salakeen' when relating this mentioned statement of Imaam Maalik, "*This means that the people of the Sunnah, do not have any general names other that this that they attribute themselves to.*" And it has been related by the reliable trustworthy Maalik Ibn Maghool, may Allaah the Most High have mercy upon him, "*If a man takes a name other than that of Islaam and of the Sunnah, then he is to be connected to that other way or religion he desires.*" And Maymoon Ibn Mahraan, may Allaah the Most High have mercy upon him, "*Be warned from every name which people take other than Islaam.*" These two narrations where mentioned by Ibn Batah, may Allaah the Most High have mercy upon him, in his work 'Al-Ibaanah as-Sughraa'.

All of these narrations are derived from the guidance of the Book of Allaah, and the Sunnah, and the way that the Companions were upon, may Allaah, the Most Glorified and the Most Exalted, be pleased with them. Allaah, the Most High, named us Muslims, and due to this there comes in the hadeeth narration on the authority of al-Haarith al-'Asharee as found in al-Musnad of Imaam Ahmad, *{Call the Muslims by their names, by that what Allaah, the Blessed and* *the Most High, has named them: Muslims, believers, worshipers of Allaah, the Blessed and the Most High.}* (Sheikh al-Albaanee has stated that this narration is authentic.)

Additionally there appeared for the people of the Sunnah other descriptive names in the pure Sharee'ah, which are synonymous to their being named as Muslims. Such as the term "Ahlus-Sunnah" which indicates their differentiation between the Sunnah and innovation in the religion, as mentioned in the hadeeth of the Prophet, , may Allaah's praise and salutations be upon him, *{...So adhere firmly to that which you know of my Sunnah and the sunnah of my rightly guided successors; and be warned from newly invented matters, as every newly invented matter in an innovation in the religion, and every innovation in the religion is misguidance.}* Due to this Imaam al-Barbahaaree, may Allaah the Most High have mercy upon him, said, "Know that Islam is the Sunnah, and the Sunnah is Islaam and one of them cannot be established without the other."

Similarly, they are also named "Ahlus-Sunnah wa al-Jama'ah" because of the statement of the Prophet, may Allaah's praise and salutations be upon him, where indicating the saved sect he said "It is the jama'ah.", this is related by Imaam Ahmad in 'al-Musnad', Imaam Abu Dawud, and others from the narration of Mua'weeyah, may Allaah, the Blessed and the Most High, be pleased with him. And similarly they are named, "the victorious group" and "the saved sect", and each one of these descriptive names has an evidence supporting it legitimacy and use.

In summary, I say regarding this practice of utilizing names, if that name being applied stands in agreement with the actual state of the individuals it is being applied to, then this is the purpose and what is intended. But if this is not the case, then applying the name while actually lacking the characteristic it indicates, does not benefit them even to the smallest degree. Of what possible benefit could applying the name "Ahlus-Sunnah wa al-Jama'ah" to the people of the sect of the 'Ash'areeyah be?? It is of no benefit to them at all. Likewise this applies to other than the sect of the 'Ash'areeyah. If the name of "Ahlus-Sunnah wa al-Jama'ah" is taken while they do not actually adhere to the beliefs and principles of the people of the Sunnah and the jama'ah, then they are not to be considered from "Ahlus-Sunnah wa al-Jama'ah". And if they persist in or still use this name "Ahlus-Sunnah wa al-Jama'ah" then it is simply an embellishment and an outward decoration.

As the criterion for distinguishing the people of the Sunnah and the Jama'ah is what was stated by Sheikh 'Abdur-Rahman as-Sa'adee, may Allaah the Most High have mercy upon him, "*Those who are truly the people of the Sunnah are those who are free from or haven't been affected by innovation in the religion, those who adhere to what the Prophet, may Allaah's praise and salutations be upon him, was upon, and what the Companions of the Prophet, were upon of the principles and fundamentals of the religion in their entirety: the principles regarding Allaah's right to be worshiped alone without any associates, the truth of prophethood, the affirmation of Allaah's decree, the required beliefs related to faith, and other similar matters.*

Whereas other than the people of the Sunnah - from the different sects of the Khawaarij, the Mu'tazilah, the Jahmeeyah, the Qadareeyah, the Rafidhah, the Murji'ah, and those later sects which were produced by and from these original first sects, all of them are considered from the people of innovated beliefs in the religion." Sheikh Sa'adee mentioned this within his rulings, may Allaah the Most High have mercy upon him.

And long before he stated this, the criterion was affirmed by Imaam al-Barberhaaree in very precise terms where he stated, may Allaah the Most High have mercy upon him, "*It is not permissible for a Muslim man to say "So and so is someone upon the Sunnah." until he has knowledge that this individual he refers to has joined together within himself the various characteristics of the Sunnah. It is not to be said that someone is upon the Sunnah until he joins and gathers upon the Sunnah in its entirety."*

Therefore the one who affirms the correct belief held by the people of the Sunnah and the Jama'ah regarding Allaah's decree, yet does not affirm what they hold regarding the principles of understanding Allaah's names and attributes, or for instance affirms their principles of understanding Allaah's names and attributes, yet does not stand upon the belief held by the people of the Sunnah and the Jama'ah regarding imaam or faith, as well as committing major sins and transgressions, or what is similar, then how could they properly be called the people of the Sunnah and the Jama'ah???

As such, that individual who truly stands upon the characteristics mentioned by Sheikh 'Abdur-Rahman as-Sa'adee, and Imaam al-Barberhaaree, may Allaah have mercy upon him, we attribute and connect him to the people of the Sunnah and categorize him as one of its people, and this is what was done by our righteous predecessors of the first generations, may Allaah, the Blessed and the Most High, have mercy upon them.

Accordingly, this condensed discussion has made apparent the evident and clear Sharee'ah foundations of attributing an individual to the belief and way they hold and proceed upon. So the one who is from the people of the Sunnah, then he is said to be "Sunnee", and the one who is from the people of innovation in the religion and adheres to desires, then similarly he is said to be from them. Depending upon of which sect or innovation he follows, he is said to be "Ash'aaree" or "Mu'tazilee'" or "Murji'ee" or "Khaarijee" or "Raafidhee" and so on.

Since this practice and its basis has been made clear, consequently know that this matter of categorization had been acted upon by the people of knowledge in practice and theory, in both the previous as well as the present age. And perhaps we will be able to present some aspects of its practical implementation in order to clarify its related objectives.

As for the theoretical aspects or principles then this is for the people of specialization from the people of knowledge, the acknowledged scholars of commendation and criticism in the religion. They have devoted themselves to this, and extensively mastered the investigation and research related to it, clarified the rulings regarding it within the Sharee'ah, and stated its fundamental principles. As for the categorization of people and their attribution to the specific beliefs they hold, the methodology they proceed upon, and the distinguishing characteristics they possess, then this is not a branch of knowledge which has been recently invented, nor is it an area of knowledge which is new; neither in regard to the Sharee'ah ruling of this practice nor its essential principles. Rather, it is the general knowledge of criticism and commendation in the affairs of the religion which the Ummah has never been distant from, but has continually remained among them, night and day.

WHO COMPLETELY REJECTS THE PRACTICE OF CATEGORIZING PEOPLE?

Therefore the one who wants, endeavors, and seeks to extinguish the light of this branch of knowledge, due to the danger it presents to his group or organization, or due to fear for his beloved leaders or speakers who have been criticized and exposed, then he is astray and leading others astray, he is himself wretched and leading other towards wretchedness!!! While the scholar who categorizes the people truthfully upon insight and wisdom due to his vigilance of preserving the religion of Allaah, the Most Perfect and the Most High, is a soldier among the soldiers of Allaah, the Most Perfect and the Most High. He disproves and refutes: matters of falsehood attributed to the religion of Allaah, the Most Exalted, the Most Magnificent, distortions of those who go to extremes, assumptions and claims of those who in reality deny Islaam, the interpretations of the ignorant, the deviations of the innovators in the religion, and the plots of the renegade sects of the Khawaarij and the others who have split away from the united ranks of the Ummah of the truthful and trustworthy prophet, may Allaah's praise and salutations be upon him.

The practice of categorization of people stands like a watchful surveillance and observation through a powerful telescope which distinguishes everyone who brings forth an innovated matter. Such that when he comes forth he then is struck by a piercing shooting star after which he is no longer able to stand, after his true state and condition has been exposed and his reality made clear, as Allaah says, ❖*..And those who do wrong will come to know by what overturning they will be overturned.*❖-(Surah Ash-Shu'ara': 227). And we could not have imagined even for a single day the striking ax of the people of desires nor their rebellious divisions would have reach this ambitious level! Such that they could strike at the guardians of the religion and it soldiers, that they could launch an attack upon this tremendous door which is from the greatest of doors of knowledge! This door being of the branch of Sharee'ah knowledge related to the criticism and commendation of individuals in relation to the religion, the door of categorizing people according to their evident affirmed beliefs and paths. And all their attempts to eliminate this branch of knowledge from the path of the Muslim Ummah, is from fear of its results upon their leaders and their established institutions!!

As the practice of categorization of people is itself from the weapons of the people of the Sunnah and the Jama'ah which, all praise is due to Allaah, the Most Exalted, the Most Magnificent, who has never weakened and will never weaken in its efforts to repress and stifle the people of innovation and desires, unveil their desires , and expose their innovations such that the people are warned from them and the Ummah recognizes those upon innovation in the religion for what they are. They act as a single hand in opposing them, striking against them, and suppressing them.

Yet it is strange that a people have come forth who attribute themselves to the Sunnah, who consider the practice of categorization permissible for themselves from any direction, or chosen purpose they wish. But as for it being employed by other than themselves, then for anyone else they see it as one of the seven dangerous sins!!! Yet they categorize people as they wish but only according to their desires, but they are not pleased with the categorization of the people of innovation in the religion, only because they follow their desires. But if one of the people of the truth correctly categorizes one of their leaders or heads with proof, then they become extremely angry, and immediately attempt to close the door of the practice of categorization and the doors of criticism and commendation in the religion in their faces of those who would speak upon proof!!!

We will bring forth an example of this which will make you both laugh and cry. All of us have heard of as-Saboonee, he is someone who is Ash'aree in his beliefs. When he published his explanation of the Qur'aan "As-Safwah" and it circulated through the different countries of the world, many of the people of knowledge, may Allaah guide them to every success, challenged its contents, exposes its realities, uncovered some of the hidden errors it contained, and warned the people against acquiring this explanation of the Book of Allaah, as the one who mistakenly relied upon it for knowledge would find that encompassed within the work was false explanations of the names and attributes of Allaah the Most Perfect and the Most High.

Yet when Sayyed Qutb came forth with his explanation of the Qur'aan, and the people of knowledge shed light on and indicated what was contained within it of false explanations of the names and attributes of Allaah, the Most Perfect and the Most High, pointed out his confused blunders in the various different areas of essential belief, mentioning some of the grievous statements that he made regarding some of the noble Companions of the Messenger of Allaah, may Allaah's praise and salutations be upon him, may Allaah, the Blessed and the Most High, be pleased with them all, and their mentioning what he stated and (check) his pen wrote of evil manners in dealing with some of the prophets of Allaah the Most Exalted, the Most Magnificent, when they mentioned these issues some of the people erupted into a wave of uproar and turmoil. They slandered those scholars who brought clarification of these mistakes, and attacked them, saying "*His books are good and beneficial! And it is obligatory that we read them.*" By your Lord, this bias is something hated, oh person of justice! As what is the difference between Sayyed Qutb and as-Saboonee, as what was done for the second was also the same as was done before for the first!!

What is the difference in the consideration of the people of knowledge and faith?? I say that as-Saboonee is in fact a hundred times better than the likes of Sayyed Qutb. As as-Saboonee simply spoke upon the same mistaken methodology of some of the people of knowledge who proceeded him, such as as-Saawee, an-Nisfee, al-Jalaalayn, and others similar to them.

But as for the one named Sayyed Qutb, he came forth with an invented and innovated approach to explaining the Book of Allaah the Most Exalted, the Most Magnificent, which the Ummah had never previously seen. His approach and path in explanation is one which combines misguided thoughts, ideas, and concepts which he embraced and believed in which were remote and separated from Islaam and completely distant. However, regarding these mistakes and statements of error they differentiate between this individual and that one. Why? What is the hidden reason for this? Because this second one is a leader of their path and their methodology! This one, Sayyed Qutb, is a sheikh of the way they are proceeding upon. Because of this they consider him beyond criticism, untouchable, and forbidden from any examination- to an extent beyond any other individual! And for the rest of the people it might be conceivable that they be connected to some innovation in the religion, or the false beliefs of the Ash'areeyah, the Mu'tazilah, the Jahmeeyah, or a similar sect. But as for him, then cease and desist! It is considered impermissible for anyone to speak regarding him! He has been surrounded by a fence of iron, which no one should dare penetrate.

This clear contradiction is an open disgrace and way of playing with the fundamentals of the religion. As it is obligatory to act with justice and turn away from personal motives, desires, hidden ambitions, and bigoted inclinations of party or group bias in the matter of this tremendous matter of Sharee'ah knowledge. As indeed the truthful Muslim scholar who properly verifies and authenticates affairs is the one who proceeds upon a single steady way and is not shaky in the matters of the religion of Allaah, the Most Perfect and the Most High.

CRITICISM AND COMMENDATION IS FOR
SPECIFICALLY FOR THE PEOPLE OF KNOWLEDGE
AND NOT FOR ONE WITH PERSONAL MOTIVATIONS
OR DESIRES

Therefore regarding knowledge of such issues related to
criticism and commendation in the religion is it necessary
that you return and seek its rulings from the people suitable
and trained for it, those who are preserved from being led
by their desires and so are impartial and unbiased in their
rulings upon individuals (male clearer). Those individuals
who have care and vigilance for the religion of Allaah the
Most Perfect and the Most High. You should not turn to
those individuals of personally oriented motivations, those
who are inconsistent, or unsteady regarding these affairs of
the religion of Allaah, the Most Perfect and the Most High.
For the purpose of giving the discussion of this subject what is
due to it, or perhaps partially putting forth what this subject
requires of explanation, I will mention in summary some of
the statements of the guiding scholar Sheikh as-Sakhaawee,
may Allaah the Most High have mercy upon him which he
mentions in his book "Fath al-Mugheeth". These statements
deal with four separate subjects:

Firstly, the importance of the branch of Sharee'ah
knowledge concerned with criticism and commendation
of individuals, and the need for both the recognition of
individuals with affirmed reliability in the religious matters
as well as those with affirmed weakness.

Secondly, a warning from working upon ones desires,
or personal motivations in this very significant area of the
religion.

Thirdly, the pressing and urgent need of this Muslim
Ummah for the utilization of the area of knowledge, and an
explanation of the evidences from the Book of Allaah and

the Sunnah which indicate its correctness and legitimacy.

Fourthly, a clarification of various doubts, or some of the misconceptions which are put forward regarding this subject or area of knowledge.

Such as the statement of some of the people that, "*The Ummah in this later age has no need to categorize the people, nor to put forth criticism and commendation of individuals in relation to the religion. Since this branch of knowledge is only required when dealing with narrators of hadeeth, there is in present times no need for it, because there are no narrators to be considered these days.*"

And as has also been said "Additionally, even for those who conveyed or transmitted knowledge of the religion previously there is no benefit in speaking about their varying conditions today. As the books have preserved and recorded this knowledge with those narrators having already been examined and spoken about to a degree that is quite sufficient."

It is the likes of these kinds of doubts and misconceptions that he clarifies, may Allaah the Most High have mercy upon him, in his book which we previous mentioned 'Fath al-Mugheeth'. Additionally, he discusses this subject even more extensively in his work 'al-Ilaam bi al-Tawbeekh Leman Dham at-Tareekh'. So the one who wishes to refer back to that beneficial work can do so. And we will now read, if Allaah so wills, what is made easy for us from what he has written or some selections from 'Fath al-Mugheeth'.

He states, in this book which is his explanation of the work 'Alfeeyah' of Sheikh al-Iraaqee, "So be warned you who is concerning yourself and working with those adhered to statements of criticism and commendation in the religion, which having transmitted from those before us clearly reflects someone's individual motivations or their desires, as following what is from either one of these will merely lead you into oppression, the swerving away from justice, abandoning fairness, false attributions, and yourself putting forth that which is undeserved from praise and commendation (make clearer).

This is from the most evil of matters that one involved in this knowledge can fall into is to be afflicted by this diseased way. And the people of the first generation were in general preserved from this, free from falling into it due to the strength and abundance of their faith. This as opposed to the people of the later times who were perhaps more likely to fall into this throughout their history. This difficulty or situation is something which is not distant from people of this religion, their methodology and ways. Since the science of criticism and commendation in the religion is a serious and significant matter, as if you commend someone without that state of reliability actually being something affirmed, then he falsely stands as someone commended without actually being reliable in this matter. Then it is feared that you yourself may be considered from that mentioned company of people who narrate a hadeeth while supposing that it might not actually be true. Similarly, if you criticize someone without obtaining the proofs supporting that, then you have put forth criticism of a Muslim according to mere opinion, and labeled him with an evil name the shame of which will remain upon his honor.'

So it should be said, despite the seriousness and weightiness of the practice of criticism and commendation of individuals, it is something which is undoubtedly necessary. That subject is another important discussion in and of itself, related to the assigning of this science to a group of scholars from within this Ummah. So again, despite the significance and seriousness of the practice of criticism and commendation of individuals, it remains something necessary for the offering of advice to the Ummah, for the Messenger, for the Book of Allaah, and to the believers. It is an obligatory right that one is rewarded for engaging in, if you enter into it intending the offering of specific advice or advice generally. The practice of criticism and commendation is from the offering of advice.

As is indicated by the statement of Imaam Ahmad, which is affirmed in the original text of Alfeeyah by al-'Iraaqee, in his statement to Abu Turab al-Nakhshabee when he censured Imaam Ahmad about speaking about people by saying, '*Do not backbite the people.*" Imaam Ahmad replied, "*What is wrong with you! This is the offering of advice, and not backbiting.*" Indeed as Allaah the Exalted says, "And say: ❰*The truth is from your Lord.* ❱-(Surah Al-Kahf: 29) Similarly, Allaah has obligated the examination and inspection of the reports brought forward by the person who is a wrongdoer as found in His statement, ❰ *If a rebellious evil person comes to you with a news, verify it* ❱-(Surah Al-Hujuraat: 6)

As found in the statement of the Prophet, may Allaah's praise and salutations be upon him, in criticizing someone, *{What an evil son of his tribe he is.}*, in his commendation of another saying, *{Certainly 'Abdullah is a righteous individual.}*, and as shown by other authentic reports about both types of individual. Due to this, such reports stand as a clear exception to that type of backbiting which is forbidden, and the Muslims stand in consensus about its acceptability. Rather, they consider it to be from the obligatory matters due to the need of the Ummah for this. From those who explicitly stated this was Imaam an-Nawawee, as well as Sheikh 'Izz Ibn 'Abdus-Salam, who stated in his work 'Qawa'id', "Speaking to expose the deficiencies of those who transmit the religion is obligatory due to what this entails of confirming what is part of our Sharee'ah, and due to what turning away from it contains of bring harm to the people through the false assertions in matters of permissibility and prohibition and other similar rulings. Likewise every type of report made permissible to accept, refer to, and rely upon by the Sharee'ah, then the bringing forth of criticism of any of those who convey it, as to their reliability, is an obligation when ruling in various affairs, due to this achieving the overall benefit of the people and preserving their rights in relation to blood, wealth and merchandise, honor and lineage, and the other established rights." The practice of speaking about different individuals is something affirmed from a number of the Companions, as well as from the generation of the Successors to the Companions of the Prophet, may Allaah's praise and salutations be upon him -as was mentioned by Imaam adh-Dhahabee; up until where he states after mentioning a number of names of those scholars of criticism and commendation who spoke regarding different people, "Indeed, how excellent was the response of Imaam Yahya Ibn Sa'eed al-Qataan to Abu Bakr Ibn Khalaad when Abu Bakr Said to him, *"Don't you fear that those individuals whose narrations you have rejected and turned away from will stand as claimants against you in from of Allaah on the day of Judgment?"* He replied, *"That those people who I have rejected stand as claimants against me is much preferred to me than the chosen Messenger, may Allaah's praise and salutations be upon him, stand as a claimant against me, due to my failure to defend the religion- meaning by this acting to restrain those who would lie and fabricate matters within his narration and the Sharee'ah he came with."*

Then Imaam as-Sakhawee stated, "Yet if it is said, and this misconception is indeed one which it is required that we take heed of and be caution about, if it is claimed that a group of the later scholars who were those experienced in the areas of history and similar fields of knowledge, such as Imaam adh-Dhahabee, and then afterwards our own sheikh, meaning Ibn Hajr al-'Asqalaanee, caused trouble and controversy by mentioning the one who made an error in a matter of the religion, even if that individual was not specifically from the people transmitting the source texts of the religion and (then?) this is from pure backbiting. Claiming this because Ibn Daqeeq al-'Eid censured Ibn as-Sama'aanee due to his mentioning some poets and speaking badly of them, when Ibn Daqeeq said,

"*If we were not compelled to speak badly about the transmitters of the religion, it would not be something permissible.*" As well as a similar statement from Ibn al-Maraabit, "*The reports have been written down, so there remains no benefit in the criticism of transmitters. Rather its need stopped at the beginning of the fourth century.*" This claim which comes from him and others who stress this who have not carefully weighed and considered their statements, finds fault with the scholars of the science of hadeeth for continuing to engage in this practice.

In refutation of this doubt and the one who puts it forth, I say, the clear justification for engaging in the practice of criticism and commendation lies in the offering of advice, and not in restricting this simply to narrators. As the reason for this practice is that continuing need to advise the Ummah, such that the ruling is related to that reason or cause. And I say, Indeed some of the possible circumstances have already been mentioned in which it is permissible to mention about someone that which he hates to have stated about him, without that being considered impermissible backbiting. Rather, in such cases it is considered an offering of advice which it is obligatory to bring forward.

Such as when the one you are mentioning has a responsibility and is not fulfilling one or more aspects of it, regardless of whether that is because he is not suitable for that, or because of intentional wrongdoing, heedlessness, or something similar. So these disliked matters are mentioned in order to enable removing that responsibility from him and placing it with another who is suitable to undertake it. Or in relation to a wrongdoer or an innovator in the religion the one who is mentioned with criticism, or what some people who deny the role of criticism and commendation absolutely wrongly refer to as impermissible backbiting. Or even there may be a wrongdoer or an innovator in the religion, and one is hesitant to speak about him despite his knowledge of him for fear of receiving harm from him if he was to expose that person's true condition.

And connected to this is criticizing the one who is somewhat lax in issuing or stating rulings, or in his categorization of the people, or in accepting testimony and transmission of information, or how he speaks about the scholars. Or the speaking about the one implicated in the issue of bribery and those involved with it, either in directly dealing with it, or simply allowing it continue when he has the ability to prevent it, or those who eat the wealth of the people through fraud and deceit, or those who take money to fabricate something related to knowledge which benefits their worldly masters, or in criticism of the one who takes power or perhaps some control of affairs less than that by means of that which is forbidden. Then in all these cases it is either permissible or even obligatory to mention him with true criticism in order to warn from the harm that comes from him. Similarly it is also obligatory to mention the one who falsely pretends to be ignorant of a matter than has been clearly stated or something similar to this, in the very first place.

Our sheikh, meaning here Ibn Hajr al-'Asqalaanee, has established and confirmed that the mentioning of all these types of individuals with criticism is within the scope of the activities of the scholar of hadeeth. And that this criticism and explanation is to be put forth by the one who is involved in properly comprehending and fulfilling these matters, as it is not for every individual to enter into and engage himself into this specialized area of knowledge. Rather it is solely for the scholars of hadeeth who are those people with knowledge of the terminologies used in criticism and recommendation, and knowledge of its principles which have already been clearly stated by the people of knowledge in general, may

Allaah the Most High have mercy upon them, and that which is further built up upon it in this area of knowledge and those like it. As it is not permissible to enter into working in this area except for the one who has fulfilled those conditions that the people of knowledge have laid down to be involved in it, meaning the regulations and guidelines of criticism and commendation in this religion.

And he has mentioned, confirmed that of all the mentioned actions are within the scope of responsibility of the scholar of hadeeth. As the foundation which has been laid down in this specific area of knowledge is the clarification of statements of criticism and commendation. Such that the one who finds fault with him, meaning the scholar of hadeeth, and mentions him with censure because of his stating the fault of the one who openly commits wrongdoing or the fault of the one who is involved with innovation in the religion or something similar; then such and individual is – and here he, meaning the Haafidh Ibn Hajr may Allaah have mercy upon him, indicates that such an individual who finds fault- is only from one of three types of person. Either he is ignorant, or someone involved in deception, or someone who shares a characteristic of the one being criticized, and so fear that they same description of fault will eventually reach him."

This concludes what we wished to transmit at this time, and hopefully it is adequate as opposed to drawing out and expanding the discussion of those scholars who are suitable to engage in criticism and commendation and explanation similar to that of examination of the issue, which would only lengthen this summarized discussion. The second half of the question from the question is: is categorization done upon conjecture?

Is categorization done upon conjecture?

So we say, that that conjecture which is known linguistically to refer to supposition, is not in its entirety blameworthy, just as it cannot be praised entirely. There is from it that which is blameworthy as well as coming from it that which is praised and accepted. Allaah, the Most Perfect and the Most High, says, ◈ *...indeed some suspicions are sins.* ◈-(Surah Al-Hujuraat: 12). And certainly Allaah, the Most Perfect and the Most High, has also named some type of doubt as knowledge in different places within His Book, as is found in His, the Most Perfect and the Most High, statement, ◈*Oh you who believe! When believing women come to you as emigrants, examine them, Allaah knows best as to their Faith, then if you ascertain that they are true believers...*◈-(Surah Al-Mumtahanah; 10)

And as is likewise found in His, the Most Exalted, the Most Magnificent, statement ◈ *we testify not except according to what we know,* ◈-(Surah Yusuf: 81). While as for the statement of Allaah, the Most Exalted, the Most Magnificent, ◈ *Certainly, conjecture can be of no avail against the truth* ◈-(Surah Yunus: 36) then what is intended here is that supposition which clearly contradicts knowledge, that being the contradiction of those who associate others with Allaah, meaning that their acts of associating others with Allaah in worship is correct and accepted, as is shown through the words, ◈ *can be of no avail against the truth...* ◈-(Surah Yunus: 36) (make easier). This indicates that it was conjecture which contradicted what was known to be true. So this type of conjecture is removed and not included or removed from the category of the blameworthy type of conjecture, as what is intended is conjecture which is equivalent to this without that doubt which has the general preponderance of being correct.

And it should also be known that many of the practical rulings of the Sharee'ah are based upon the general preponderance of being correct, this is something recognized by the people of knowledge and their students. Indeed, the majority of the principles of the Sharee'ah are built upon this, as is seen in the principle of seeking the overall benefit and avoiding the overall harm, this is based upon accepted types of conjecture.

Therefore the people of knowledge acknowledge that considered conjecture is of three types, that conjecture which is of the lowest level, that of the highest level, and that which is of a middle level. This was affirmed by Sheikh al-'Izz Ibn 'Abdus-Salaam, may Allaah the Most High have mercy upon him. The benefit derived from this precise division returns back to when there is a conflict between the highest level of conjecture and middle and lower types, the highest takes precedence over the other two below it. Just as if there is a contradiction between conjecture of the middle level with that conjecture of the type below it, the middle level takes precedence, and so forth. Therefore if this is understood, then what are we saying is intended when we speak about categorizing the people by conjecture??

If the doubt presented is similar or on the equal level of credibility as what is affirmed about someone, then it is not correct to consider it and it is upon us to turn away from it due to the statement of the Prophet, may Allaah's praise and salutations be upon him, *{Beware of conjecture, as indeed conjecture is from the most deceitful of speech.}*

Yet if that doubt or conjecture is of a level that requires it to be considered within the Sharee'ah and is that information which reaches the level of a general probability of being correct, then this information is used in determining the categorization of individuals, and the people of knowledge, may Allaah the Most High have mercy upon them, do not found any fault in this. Due to this if you examine the methodology of the first generations in the area of criticism and commendation of individuals, and speaking about the people of innovation, you see that that they gave consideration to this considered or valid type of conjecture.

So for example, some of them stated, "*The one who is able to conceal from us his innovation, he cannot conceal from us his companionship.*" meaning that we know about him according to the one whom he sits with, even if he does not reveal his innovation in the religion through his explicit statements and actions.

Yahya Ibn Sa'eed al-Qahtaan , may Allaah the Most High have mercy upon him, said, "*When Sufyaan at-Thawree came to Basrah. ar-Rabee'a Ibn Sabeeh was seen to have position, status, and standing among the people. As such Sufyan at-Thawree asks about his affair, and inquired about his condition and what he was upon. He asked, "What is his way?" They replied to him that his way was that of the Sunnah.*" Then he asked, "*Who are his close associates*"? They answered, "*They are people involved in the innovation of the denial of Allaah's qadr.*" He then said, "*Then he himself is a Qadaree.*" Ibn Batah, may Allaah the Most High have mercy upon him, commented on this narration saying, "*He made this statement in wisdom, and was indeed correct. And he spoke with knowledge that conforms to the Book of Allaah and the Sunnah, and that which indicates the wisdom he possessed, by perceiving what was to there to be recognized, understood what would be comprehended by the people of true insight and clarification. As Allaah the Most Exalted, the Most Magnificent, has said ۞ Oh you who believe! Take not as your advisors, consultants, protectors, helpers, friends, those outside your religion since they will not fail to do their best to corrupt you. ۞-(Surah Al-Imran: 118)*"

So the student of knowledge should know that a great deal of the categorization of individuals by the people of knowledge in the past and present ages, is upon a foundation of accepted considered and valid conjecture. As for that categorization, which is only based upon indisputable absolute information, than this is something occurring rarely within this Ummah.

So categorization by acceptable considered conjecture, is similar to categorization based upon the testimony given by two just individuals for someone that he is from the people of desires and innovation and judging him according to that. Moreover that categorization done according to secondary indications and what is similar to it- is from the matters which are based upon acceptable conjecture just as is done with many of the rulings of the Sharee'ah of Islaam.

CONCLUSION

So in closing this discussion, I say that it is necessary for the student of knowledge to be wary and cautious about this delving into this area of knowledge of criticism and commendation, and be very cautious with a severe cautious such that he stay far from entering into this area of knowledge when only a beginning student of knowledge. Because this area of knowledge is difficult to proceed in, and difficult to progress within. Such that a sign of a student of knowledge being granted success in the beginning of his efforts is that he occupy himself with the memorization of knowledge based texts, and that he devote himself to memorizing, understanding, studying, and reviewing them, and what is similar to this. Just as a sign of his failure to be granted success is his being found to be occupied with these advanced areas of knowledge in the initial states of his turning to seek knowledge. Therefore the student of knowledge should turn away from concentrating on this area of knowledge in the initial period of his seeking knowledge, and devote himself to the fundamentals of knowledge, until such a time that Allaah grants him general success in that, if Allaah so wills. and Allaah , the Most High, knows best, may the praise and blessing be upon prophet Muhammad.

(2)

A CLARIFICATION FROM SHEIKH SAALEH AL-FAUZAAN REGARDING THE METHODOLOGY OF THE PEOPLE OF THE SUNNAH AND THE JAMA'AH IN REFUTING THE PEOPLE OF INNOVATION IN THE RELIGION &

A CLARIFICATION REGARDING THE VALUE OF THE BOOKS OF REFUTATION PRODUCED THE EARLIER GENERATIONS

,

Sheikh Fauzaan, may Allaah preserve him, said in a section entitled, "*The Methodology of the People of the Sunnah and the Jama'ah in Refuting the People of Innovation in the Religion*" within the work "*The Guidance of the true Belief*" (page 383),

The methodology of Ahlus-Sunnah wal-Jamaa'ah in refuting the people of innovation in the religion is based upon the Book of Allaah and the Sunnah. This is a methodology that is both convincing and persuasive, such that it refutes the doubts of the innovators and their misconceptions. We derive from the Qur'aan and Sunnah the obligation of holding firmly to the established practices of the Messenger, and striving against innovation in the religion and newly introduced matters. There have been many works written in this area. In the books related to correct beliefs there are general refutations of the sects of the Shee'ah, the Khawaarij, the Jahmeeyah, the Mu'tazilah, and the 'Ashareeyah, opposing their innovated statements in the fundamentals of the faith and belief. The people of the Sunnah wrote books specifically in this area of refutation, such as the book written by Imaam Ahmad '*Radd 'Ala Jahmeeyah*"; and other leading scholars composed work of this type. For example, that written by Uthman Ibn Saeed Ad-Daramee, as well as the books of Sheikh al-Islaam Ibn Taymeeyah and his student Ibn Qayyim. Additionally, there is Sheikh Muhammad Ibn Abdul-Wahaab and others who refuted these sects, as well as refuting those who worship at graves and followers of Sufism. So from the books specifically written in refutation of the people of innovation in the religion, there are indeed many. For example among the earlier written works are books such as:

The book *al-'Itisaam*" by Imaam ash-Shaatabee.

The book "*Iqtidaa as-Siraat al-Mustaqeem*" by Sheikh al-Islaam Ibn Taymeeyah, as he has devoted a significant portion of it to the refutation of the innovators.

The book *"'Inkaar al-Hawaadith wa al-Bid'ah* " by Ibn Wadhaah

The book *"al-Hawaadidh wa Bid'ah"* by at-Tartooshee

The book *"al-Baaith Alaa Inkaar al-Bid'ah wa al-Hawadith"* of Abee Shaamah

And from the modern works on this subject:

The book *"al-Ibdaa' Fe Madhar al-Ibtidaa'"* by Sheikh Alee Mafoudh

The book *"As-Sunnan wa Mubtadiaat al-Mutaliqat bi Inkar wa al-Salawaat"* by Sheikh Muhammad Ibn Ahmad al-Shaqarah al-Hawandee.

The work *"at-Tadheer min al-Bid'ah"* by Sheikh 'Abdul-'Azeez Ibn Baaz

So the scholars of the Muslims have not ceased, and all praise is due to Allaah, from criticizing innovation and refuting the innovators in the religion by means of newspapers, magazines, and other media, as well as by Friday sermons, conferences, and lectures. Through such means as these there has been a significant enlightenment of the Muslims, and a suppression of innovation in the religion, and a subduing of those who innovate in the religion.

Additionally he, may Allaah preserve him, said in his work entitled, *"An Explanation of the Mistakes of Some Writers"*: page 132:

From Where Do We Obtain Beneficial Knowledge

Beneficial knowledge is obtained from the Book of Allaah and the Sunnah, through understanding them, contemplating them, and carefully studying them, seeking the assistance in this from the books written about worshiping Allaah alone, those which gather transmitted explanations the Book of Allaah, those containing explanation the meaning of hadeeth narrations, those books which have gathered the rulings in the religion and their principles, as well the books of grammar and the Arabic language. However, it is necessary that a warning be given about a grave deception and scheme which has spread among the youth from the hands of some of the people of bias and partisanship who have come to be known as "guides" and as "thinkers"; and many of the youth have been diverted and turned away from those beneficial books. This deception is found in their statements regarding the books which explain Allaah's right to be worshipped alone, those books which encompass and explain the methodology of the righteous first generations of Muslims and those who followed and adhered to their way in the matters of understanding Allaah's names and attribute, those books which contain refutations of the false negation of the sect of the Jahmeeyah and the Mu'tazilah and those that they gave rise to, those books which contain the explanations of the necessity of directing all worship towards Allaah alone, and what contradicts this completely and what diminishes it from different aspects of associating others in that worship.

Regarding these early books they say: [These old books only refute people who have long since passed away and are now gone. They discuss misconceptions which have ceased to exist. We must abandon these books and occupy ourselves with refuting the new deviant methodologies such as Communism, Ba'thist Socialism...] until the end of what they mention. As they say regarding the books of ruling and jurisprudence what is similar to: [These are very complex books, and they incorporate suppositions which are far from reality, so we should abandon them and derive solutions to our problems directly from the Book of Allaah and the Sunnah ...] to the end of what they state.

The response to that has several aspects:

1. Certainly, if we abandoned these books we would not have the ability to refute these newly emerging ideologies. These books instruct us in the proper methodology of refutation, and the correct way of reasoning and argumentation. Therefore if we abandoned them we would be in the position of the one who drops his weapon and then proceeds to meet the enemy without a weapon. Then what will result from this?! Truly, only your defeat and destruction or being captured.

2. Certainly the sects and groups which were refuted by the books of the early scholars which clarify the issues regarding Allaah's right to be worshiped alone have not ceased to exist. Rather, they have present day followers who embrace and adhere to what those first groups were upon, from the issues of negating Allaah's names and attributes, or the distortion of them, or engaging in actions which are associating others in the worship due to Allaah alone. These followers speak about these matters and spread them in their own publications as well as through comments on the printed works of others. So how can it be said that these sects have ceased to exist?!

3. As for the presumption and claim that these deviant groups have ceased to exist and there is no longer anyone who follows them, then the misconceptions and misinterpretations which caused them to go astray are present in the books they left behind; and what is feared is that one may come across these writings from the hands of those who do not understand their reality, and then go astray due to this, or this happens by the hands of those are clearly misguided and the people then are misguided by them. Therefore the study of what opposes these misconceptions and clarifies their falsehood from the early books of Ahlus-Sunnah wa'al-Jama'ah is something which is required.

4. The modern deviated methodologies and paths are descended from the early deviated methodologies and paths which the previous scholars have refuted in their books; therefore if we understand the earlier form of falsehood, then we also understand the falsehood which descended and was born out of it.

5. As for the assumption or claim that these new deviated methodologies do not have an origin in the past, then even if this was the case there is no conflict or contradiction between the refutation of the first forms of falsehood and refutation of the new forms of falsehood, in order that we not be deceived by either one of them! As it is obligatory to refute falsehood whenever one is able, the new and the old. And Allaah, the Exalted mentioned in the Qur'aan those aspects of disbelief the first people possessed as well as well as what was possessed by the first people, and refuted all of the them.

6- As for their statements regarding the books of jurisprudence and fiqh, that "They are structured in a very complex way, and have strange suppositions." Then this is correct, if one speak truthfully about some of these texts due to being summarized, as they have been summarized in their explanations and clarifications, so the complexity is removed.

As for the strange suppositions, then these are regarding theoretical problems if they were to occur, a valuable resource for this Ummah, derived from the sources of the Book of Allaah and the Sunnah, which should not be undervalued or disdained.

So, the books of our predecessors of the first generations are resources which it is obligatory that we safeguard and that we must benefit from; not being deceived by the schemes of the enemies of Islaam and the partisans who are displeased and saddened by what is found within these books from clarification of the truth and the refutation of falsehood which they have inherited from their predecessors from the Jahmeeyah and the Mu'tazilah. So they begin stirring up the youth concerning them, instigating and working up amongst them an aversion and dislike for these books. ◈ *They want to extinguish Allaah's Light with their mouths* ◈ -(Surah Tawbah:32) However, there has never ceased to be, and all praise is due to Allaah, those always present, the people of truth who were not deceived by this deceitful propaganda which opposes their illustrious history.

Allaah has decreed for these lands, and all praise is due to Allaah, Islamic universities which have been established upon teaching Islamic heritage, reviving and spreading it. They take as their model of educational methodology the verifying of the books which teach the methodology of the first generations of Muslims, as well as their printing and distribution. Examples are the Islamic university of Muhammad Ibn Saud, and the Islamic University in Medinah, and the Islamic University Umm al-Quraa, and likewise what has been established through other universities in the kingdom of Saudi Arabia and other countries from praiseworthy efforts in this area.

(3)

CLARIFICATION FROM SHEIKH MUQBIL IBN HAADEE AL-WAADIEE, MAY ALLAAH HAVE MERCY UPON HIM REGARDING THE POSITIONS OF TWO GROUPS OF PEOPLE IN REGARD TO WARNING AND REFUTATIONS

Question: *Certainly we have recently become engrossed with the controversy which has occurred between Sheikh al-Albaanee and Sheikh Bakr Abu Zayd, may Allaah preserve them both. Likewise also that which has occurred between Sheikh al-Albaanee and Zaheer as-Shawaysh, may Allaah preserve both of them. So should we, as was done previously, simply sit with the youth in order teach them the general matters of the religion, or should we instead clarify these doubts and various issues which have now arisen and are focused upon due to what has occurred?*

Answer: As for those differences between the people of knowledge which do not enter into the realm of criticism in relation to an aspect of correct beliefs, then it is necessary, as was done in the past, to put it in its proper place. Additionally, I advise the students of knowledge to devote themselves wholeheartedly to seeking knowledge and to avoid paying attention to these types of issues which are not of significant harm. Do not absorb yourself with having biased support towards so and so nor towards so and so. Rather devote yourself to seeking knowledge. As on one occasion a brother wrote to me from Mecca and said to me, "*This biased and divisive partisanship is spreading dangerously here among us. So what should we do?*" So I advised him, by saying, "Dedicate your selves with a full devotion towards seeking knowledge and do not pay attention to these matters." As the one who involves himself and wishes to refute these matters is made to suffer. I said to him, "Do not occupy yourself with refuting them, you are a student of knowledge, and are in need of increasing yourself in knowledge. And if you occupy yourself with these matters it will preoccupy you from memorizing the Qur'an and obtaining beneficial knowledge. Therefore do not occupy yourself with these affairs, but dedicate yourself wholeheartedly toward committing yourself to acquiring beneficial knowledge.

As we are concerned with teaching the common people and others, not worried about whether so and so is correct and so and so is in error, and so and so is such and such. Rather, we concern ourselves with teaching the people the correct beliefs and with teaching them the guidance of the Book of Allaah and the Sunnah of the Messenger of Allaah, may Allaah's praise and salutations be upon him, and that which they are required to learn of the Arabic language, and what they need to understand from the terminology of the hadeeth sciences. When we visited Egypt, the young brothers also wanted to occupy us in this way. Every group of brothers sent two or three brothers to explain and convince me about their view and positions in these affairs. But I said to them, "I am very busy, so we will all seek knowledge for a year, and then after that time, if Allaah so wills, we will delve into these various issues. As you are only destroying your time, preoccupying you minds, and disturbing your intellects in this way. The Messenger of Allaah, may Allaah's praise and salutations be upon him, said in a hadeeth narrated in Jaame'a at-Tirmidhee on the authority of Abee Amaamah, *{ A people have not gone astray after having been upon guidance except through their entering into disputes and controversies.}* Then the Messenger of Allaah, may Allaah's praise and salutations be upon him, recited the verse ﴾ *And say: "Are our gods better or is he ('Isaa)?" They quoted not the above example except for argument. No! But they are a quarrelsome people.*﴿ - (Surah az-Zukhruf: 58). And this way leads to malice within one's heart towards your Muslim brother who is righteous. And you don't know, perhaps your heart will come to have malice against your brother simply due to this disputing and arguing."

[Source: "Ghaarat al-Ashreetah", vol. 1 page 73]

Question: *Why don't you speak and put forth your criticism of the people of this modern age who are weak or should be abandoned, using the same kind or a similar type of criticism utilized by the scholars of the early centuries? You might say for instance, "So and so is Hizbee and weak, so do not take from him." or "So and so is a liar or is an obvious deceiver" or "He is to be abandoned", or using other terms, along with making clear the false methodology of the one you are speaking against in relation to his Shi'ism, or Sufism, or Hizbeeyah, or his weakening the methodology of the first generations?*

Answer: This would be something good, however I am busy, and have efforts that I must be concerned with. And I want to complete these other efforts, as I view them as more beneficial. For example, my work *"The Scholars of Imaam al-Haakim"* or fully *"The Scholars of the Scholars of Imaam al-Haakim and the Narrators He Relied upon in His Work al-Mustradrak Whose Biographies Cannot be Found in Tahdheeb at-Tahdheeb"* or such as my striving to complete the work *"The Authentic Connected Narrations Not Found Within the Two Saheeh Books of Imaams al-Bukhaaree and Muslim Arranged According to their Narrators"* or such as my work *"The Authentic Collection of Narrations Not Found Within the Two Saheeh Books of Imaams al-Bukhaaree and Muslim"* So I am clearly busy, and I find that I have become lacking in many other activities.

How many different books are sent to us from here and there where the brothers who sent them say, *"We need you to refute this."* So I say, "If I am able to do so I will do so, but only by recording my response on an audio cassette. Because I am busy with other matters which I hold are more beneficial to Islaam and the Muslims."

Additionally, there is my work, "*The Exit from the Trial*", and "*The Struggle*" and "*Bridling the Resistant One, & Preventing the Malicious And Jealous Ones*" I consider them to be works of criticism and commendation in the religion. Indeed, we have spoken in the book "*The Struggle*" about the Sufees, about the foolish ones found here in Yemen, about the sect of the Mukaaramah, and those involved in what is put forth in the newspapers of falsehood, as well as many of those callers who are calling to biased and divisive partisanship between the people.

Also the work "*Bridling the Resistant One...*" within it we have spoken about the Yemenee political organization, "Islaah", which is upon the methodology of the Ikhwaan al-Muslimeen, as well as those different groups who have submitted and bound themselves to a specific "foundation" or "charitable organization". Therefore I myself consider these as works of criticism and commendation in the religion.

Yet after stating that, I advise my brothers to devote themselves wholeheartedly to seeking knowledge. As this focus on differences which are present in the land of the two holy cities and in Najd between some of the people of knowledge, arise from not being occupied and the free time which results from that. As how easy it is for you to simply remember statements such as, "So and so is Hizbee" and "So and so is only a government agent" and then to go back and forth from one sitting to another. Rather what I want from you is that you start with the memorization of the Qur'an along with what you are able to undertake of the memorization of the narrations of the Messenger of Allaah, may Allaah's praise and salutations be upon him, and the study of the Arabic language.

So I say, these controversies which spring up among you result from lack of activity and unoccupied time, such that the people come to be pleased with such statements- or even if they are not pleased with them to be occupied by them. Because if you occupied yourselves with the memorization of the Qur'an, and with obtaining beneficial knowledge, then you would not find time to even consider such statements. Indeed, someone brought news to me from the land of the two holy cities and in Najd, such that he said "Sheikh so and so said and Sheikh so and so said, and Sheikh so and so said,..." I said to the one speaking, "Oh so and so,

He has thrown upon you their yells and shouts stolen from his own rooms,

> *So give me a hadeeth narration, not the talk of the travelers!*

Moreover, I want to test you as to the knowledge and information that you have taken from your studies with us, and what you have come to possess." So that individual who had transmitted that news just scratched his head, and became silent. So be warned against wasting and squandering your time in these matters. Rather, you should put forth strong efforts and struggles in obtaining beneficial knowledge, and acquiring and understanding of the religion of Allaah. And any matter that comes to us which contradicts the Book of Allaah and the Sunnah of the Messenger of Allaah, may Allaah's praise and salutation be upon him and his family, then indeed we abandon it and reject it.

[Source, "Ghaarat al-Ashreetah", vol. 2 page 410-411]

Question: *We observe that some of those who affiliate themselves with the methodology of the first three generations choose to occupy themselves with criticism and warning from the astray groups and sects, but neglect the seeking of knowledge, whereas others who claim the same methodology do give priority to seeking knowledge yet turn away from the matter of warnings and criticisms. Such that it has reached the state where those of the second group say, "Certainly, criticizing is not from the methodology of the people of the Sunnah at all." So what is correct in this issue?*

Answer: As for those who only occupy themselves with critically examining the mistakes of others and warning from them- they can be considered disproportionate in their affairs of seeking knowledge, as found in the answers to the questions of our brothers from the Emirates, as well as being excessive in focusing on the realm of criticism. As what is seen or observed when one considers the lives of our previous scholars? If we look at the biography of Ibn Abee Haatim, we find that he was a tremendous memorizer; indeed he was even given the title of Sheikh al-Islaam. The same case can be seen with Imaam al-Bukhaaree, Imaam Ahmad Ibn Hanbal, Yahya Ibn Ma'een, Yahya Ibn Sa'ed al-Qahtaan, Abu Haatim, Abu Zura'ah, ad-Darqutnee, Ibn Hibaan, and Haakim. They authored many beneficial books, such as in the subject of the explanations of the Qur'an, as well as works in the various hadeeth sciences. They produced beneficial works and preserved for us the Sunnah of the Messenger of Allaah, may Allaah's praise and salutations be upon him and his household.

But in addition they also produced beneficial books related to criticism and commendation of individuals in the religion. Therefore it is necessary that we join between the first focus and priority and the second, as otherwise an individual will be deficient from one aspect, as well as being excessive from another.

As I ask you, according to what criterion or scale will we assess or judge the state of individuals if we are ignorant of beneficial knowledge? Will we simply judge them by our desires or by following what has been said to you by sheikh so and so? Such that if Sheikh so-and-so recants a position you also recant it, and if he holds a position regarding a number of individuals then you also hold it. Therefore it can be seen that it is required that we combine between the first matter and the second.

As for the second group which was mentioned, those who only give attention to knowledge without raising their heads towards commending or criticizing anyone, then in my view, of the two groups overall they are in a better state than the first group. Because the first mentioned group is attempting to enter into or concern themselves with that area which it is not within their present ability to confront personally. Yet despite this fact, it is clear that this second group has itself torn down or subverted an important aspect of Islaam. Indeed, that work of our brother Bakr Ibn 'Abdullah Abu Zayd "*Categorizing the People between Doubt and Certainty*" in this subject, should be considered the worst book from those which he authored. On the other hand many of his works, all praise is due to Allaah, are from the best of those available, may Allaah reward him with good.

But as for the destruction of the role or position of criticizing and commending in the religion, then know that Allaah the Most Glorified and Most Exalted has Himself has said in His Noble Book, ﴾ *And do not obey every worthless habitual swearer and scorner, going about with malicious gossip - A preventer of good, transgressing and sinful, Cruel, moreover, and an illegitimate pretender.* ﴿-(Surah al-Qalam: 10-13) And He said, ﴾ *Perish the two hands of Abu Lahab and perish he! His wealth and his children will not benefit him!*

He will be burnt in a Fire of blazing flames! And his wife too, who carries wood. Around her neck is a twisted rope of fiber. ❧-(Surah al-Masad: 1-5). Allaah, the Most Perfect and the Most High, has criticized Abu Lahab and also criticized his wife. Likewise Musa when he intended to strike or beat the one with him from the previous incident of killing, said to him.❧ *Indeed, you are an evident, persistent deviator.*❧ These are all evidence of the permissibility of legitimate criticism of someone.

And the Prophet, may Allaah's praise and salutations be upon him and his household, said regarding a man who came to sit with him, { *What an evil man of the tribe he is.}* But when that man entered, he sat with him and spoke with him nicely. Such that 'Aishah asked why he did that after having criticized him, and he replied, { *The worst people, in the sight of Allaah are those whom the people abandon to save themselves from their foul language. }* This is narrated in both Saheeh al-Bukhaaree and Saheeh Muslim on the authority of 'Aishah.

It is also narrated in Saheeh al-Bukhaaree from the hadeeth of 'Aishah, that one of the women from the household of Abu Sufyan said, "Abu Sufyaan is a man who is miserly, not giving us what is sufficient." Yet the Prophet, may Allaah's praise and salutations be upon him and his household, remained silent regarding her criticism of Abu Sufyan. Moreover, in another instance the Prophet, may Allaah's praise and salutations be upon him and his household, asked, { *Who is your chief, oh Banu Salaamah?" They replied al-Jad Ibn Qays, yet we see him to be a miser." So the Prophet, may Allaah's praise and salutations be upon him and his household, said, "So which disease is worse than miserliness? Rather, your chief is 'Amr Ibn al-Jamooh."}* And the Prophet, may Allaah's praise and salutations be upon him and his household, said to Muadh Ibn Jabal, "*Are you a trial for the people, oh Mua'dh?!*" And he said to Abu Dhar,

{ Indeed you are a man who has some aspects of those days of ignorance before Islaam still within him.} And he said to some of the women of his household, *{Indeed, you are like some of the evil women who tempted Prophet Yusuf.}* This was narrated by Imaam al-Bukhaaree in his Saheeh. And the Prophet, may Allaah's praise and salutations be upon him and his household, said, *{ I do not believe that so and so and so and so understands anything at all from our religion.}* Laith Ibn Sa'd explained this as referring to two of the hypocrites who did not truly embrace Islaam.

And the Prophet, may Allaah's praise and salutations be upon him and his household, said to Hamal Ibn Maalik Ibn an-Naabighah in judgment when it occurred that a woman from his people struck another woman with something which caused the other woman to abort the unborn child she was carrying. So the Prophet said, *{ "They should be given a male or a female slave in compensation." So Hamal Ibn Maalik Ibn an-Naabighah said, "Oh Messenger of Allaah, why should we pay for that which has never eaten nor drunk anything, nor was even born. One such as this should not be considered." So the Prophet, may Allaah's praise and salutations be upon him and his household, said, "This one is from the brothers of the magicians"}*, due to his arguing using rhymed poetry.

And the Prophet, may Allaah's praise and salutations be upon him and his household, said, *{ The extremists are destroyed, The extremists are destroyed, The extremists are destroyed. }* And he said regarding the sect of the Khawaarij, *"Indeed, they are the dogs of the Hellfire."* He also said, *{ Indeed, they will pass through the religion the way an arrow passes through the animal that was shot at. }*

Therefore the one who is deficient in implementing criticism and commendation in the religion, is then deficient in implementing an aspect of the Sunnah. If criticism and commendation are not implemented then everyone speaks claiming to be a "caller to Allaah" or an "esteemed scholar", such as is seen in the speech of 'Alee at-Tantaawee, or the speech of Mahmood as-Sawaaf, or the speech of Muhammad al-Ghazaalee, or the speech of Hassan at-Turaabee, or the speech of as-Sharaawee, or the speech of the different Shee'ah and Rawaafidh, or such as the speech of the Sufee -Hasan Saqqaaf.

Therefore I say- no one knowingly turns away from understanding of this branch of knowledge except an individual who is ignorant, or an individual with a spiteful heart, or an individual who comes to know that he has himself been criticized. So he then has an aversion to criticism and commendation in the religion due to the fact that he learns that he has been publicly criticized. Yet Allaah rejects anything other than what brings victory to His religion and makes supreme His word, and brings forth the truth. Such that the people of the Sunnah have now given priority to criticism and commendation for the sake of the religion, And before it was as if some of them were sleeping, so Allaah facilitated for them those people those who would awaken them. As before some of them didn't used to speak extensively in matters of commendation and criticism- as if this was something specific to the period of Imaam al-Bukhaaree and Muslim.

But I say clearly, shouldn't we criticize the one in this age who says, "Popular Democracy is compatible with Islaam."? In reality, is not the correct way that we criticize the one who makes such a false claim and we strive to explain to the people that the one who makes this claim is a deceiver from the many deceivers? Shouldn't we criticize those individuals who speak against and attack the scholars of the Muslims? Additionally, how could we, as we do, criticize our own esteemed scholars in some knowledge-based issues, yet consider it proper that we remain silent about these more significant matters?!?

Therefore it is necessary that we join between these two matters, and focus both on seeking knowledge as well as the criticism and warning against those who have opposed the truth. As when we read the biographies of the Companions and read the biographies of the Successors to the Companions as well as those of the generation that followed them –the Successors of those Successors, we find that they often made statements that reflected this. Where do we stand when we hear the statements of Imaam ad-Dhahabee, "*Zatn, who is Zatn? He is only is a deceiver from among the deceivers, claiming that he is a Companion six hundred years after the year of the Hijra!*" Or when we hear the likes of the statements of Imaam as-Sha'afee who said, "*Narrating on Haram Ibn 'Uthmaan is itself haraam (forbidden).*" Or another statement from Imaam as-Sha'afee, "*The one who narrates on al-Bayaadhee (meaning a person of whiteness), may Allaah make his eyes white with blindness.*" Where do we stand when we hear such statements? Do we say that Imaam as-Sha'afee is from those who are harsh and unnecessarily severe, someone who was wrong in his speaking against the Muslims or in speaking about those scholars?

We challenge you to prove with evidence that we have falsely spoken against any of the scholars, or against those advocating popular Democracy, or those who speak from this personal opinion or that personal opinion, or those who affirm the various mandates and resolutions of the United Nations or that of the Council of Nations, or those who say; "This age is not one of saying "so and so informed me" and "so and so narrated to me", nor of stating that this narration is authentic or this one is weak." And we respond to this last by saying, rather, indeed this is certainly the age for this, as many hadeeth narrations presently circulating among the people are either weak or fabricated. I conclude what I have said with what was mentioned by al-Haafidh as-Sooree, may Allaah have mercy upon him. Where he said:

> *Say to the one who opposes narrations of hadeeth and*
>> *comes forth blaming the people of hadeeth and*
>> *those who adhere to them,*
>
> *Do you say this to me based upon knowledge, my son*
>> *or does it come from ignorance, as ignorance is*
>> *the character of a fool.*
>
> *Do you blame those who strive to preserve the religion?*
>> *-from falsehoods, lies, and distortions,*
>
> *and find fault with their statements while what they narrate*
>> *is referred to by every true scholar and those*
>> *with understanding of the religion?*

And I do not intend through this that the one upon the Sunnah should unnecessarily occupy his time with this. Rather one should occupy some of his time with clarifying the mistakes of the various sects and groups, and a good portion of his time for easy breathing and necessary rest, and also some time for eating and drinking, and so on. Indeed, what I intend is that one be as has been said:

> *A man stands with his feet firmly upon the earth,*
>> *but indeed the highest of his goals is in the stars.*

Some of our brothers in Islaam have written to me and said, "Do not preoccupy yourself with these matters." They incorrectly believe that I am preoccupied with these matters, while in fact, all praise is due to Allaah, I am not. My efforts of composition and writing have their own time, as do my classes given in order to teach the people, and matters of criticism and commendation of individuals for the sake of the religion also has its place and time. Ibn Jawzee confronted the people of his time because of their using and narrating weak or fabricated hadeeth, and this practice is similarly present today. Likewise, others besides him from the scholars of the first generations confronted the people of their ages regarding the use of weak or fabricated narrations, and similarly people who engage in this are undoubtedly present today.

Yet, all praise is due to Allaah, the knowledge of the Sunnah has spread tremendously, such that even the "Bankrupt Brotherhood" (the Muslim Brotherhood organization) is now teaching the science of hadeeth terminology! However as is said:

> *They praise the efforts of the guard, yet he acts only for the sake of trying,*
>> *to retain in those young men already among them- so that they do not run away.*

Look at 'Abdullah Sa'tar from their group who has taken up the book "Sharh at-Tahaweeyah" and it now teaching it. Oh 'Abdullah Sa'tar, you have certainly undertaken a difficult ascent! So what occurred is that on the first night of those classes there was a large group of people attending, and the second night there were less, and on the third night even less. Thereafter, there were perhaps only seven people present, and then later maybe three.

Because in terms of knowledge, he actually doesn't have a firm grasp of matters except to know that such and such was said in the newspaper "al-Hayaat", and that such and such was mentioned by the "London Broadcast", and that such and such paper mentioned this or that. Therefore it is clear through their efforts, that what they desire is only that their youth remain with them and not abandon them. So they announce: "We are teaching the issues of belief!" "We are teaching hadeeth terminology!", and so forth and so on. However we see regarding them, as it is said, "*Haleemah turned from her previous ways, but when they saw that this way neither benefited nor profited them, they returned once again to lies and deception*".

[*Advices & Clarifications: pages 111- 117*]

(4)

CLARIFICATION FROM SHEIKH AHMAD AN-NAJMEE, MAY ALLAAH HAVE MERCY UPON HIM, THAT ADVISING THE MUSLIMS THROUGH REFUTATIONS IS FROM THE WAY OF THE FIRST GENERATIONS OF MUSLIMS.

All praise is due to Allaah, praise and salutations be upon the Messenger of Allaah, upon his household, and his Companions. As for what follows:

Through the examination of the conditions and situations of various individuals it can be recognized that there is a group of people who attribute themselves to the way of the Salaf, according to their claim; however they are those who dislike refutations and the clarification of people's errors. They see them as the cause of separation, the spreading of ill will and bitter feelings among the people, a cause for the growth of enmity, and the sowing of the seeds of division among them. But this perspective indicates their lack of a comprehensive understanding of what is produced and what results from each of the two ways, meaning either to refute and clarify or to abandon refutation, from their good or evil results, as well as the sweetness or bitterness born from them.

And in reality, refuting the one who has differed with the Book and the Sunnah is considered an aspect of forbidding wrongdoing which is outward and apparent, and refuting falsehoods that are being promoted among the people. Moreover Allaah has joined this matter of enjoining the good and forbidding wrongdoing with one's faith. And He has made the three of them matters leading to the well being of the Ummah. *You Muslims are the best of peoples ever raised up for mankind; you enjoin the good and forbid wrongdoing, and you believe in Allaah.* -(Surah Aal-'Imraan: 110) Ibn Katheer, may Allaah have mercy upon him, stated in his book 'Tafseer al-Qur'an al-Adheem' regarding this verse, "Allaah the Exalted has informed us that this Ummah of Muhammad is the best of all nations. He has said, *You are the best of peoples ever raised up for mankind*. Imaam al-Bukhaaree stated that Muhammad Ibn Yusuf narrated on the authority of Sufyaan on the authority of Abu Meseerah on the authority of Abu Haazem from Abu Hurairah, may Allaah be pleased with him, that he said regarding the verse: *You (Muslims) are the best of peoples ever raised up for mankind.* ﴾ "This means the best of peoples towards the people, as you bring them with chains on their necks until they embrace Islaam." This same explanation was given by Ibn 'Abbas, Mujaahid, Ikrimah, Atta' and ar-Rabee'a Ibn Anas. Atta' al-'Awfee said ﴾**You Muslims are the best of peoples ever raised up for mankind.** ﴿ meaning the best of peoples towards the people. And the meaning of the statement that they are the best of nations, is that they are the most beneficial of people towards the people. Because of this, it is immediately followed by ﴾ *you enjoin the good and forbid wrongdoing, and you believe in Allaah*﴿ .

Then Ibn Katheer said, *"Imaam Ahmad said Ahmad Ibn 'Abdul-Maalik narrated to us that Shareek narrated to us on the authority of Samaak from 'Abdullah Ibn 'Ameerah from the husband of Darrah Bint Abu Lahab from Darah Bint Abu Lahab who said: A man stood up in front of the Messenger of Allaah, may Allaah's praise and salutations be upon him, while he was on the minbar and said, 'Oh Messenger of Allaah, which of the people is the best?' The Messenger of Allaah, may Allaah's praise and salutations be upon him, said, { **The best of the people are those who are most proficient in recitation, those greatest in the fear of Allaah, and those strongest in enjoining the good, those strongest in forbidding wrongdoing, and those who are best in keeping ties with their families.**} ... Then Ibn Katheer brings forth many narrations which show the merits of this Ummah saying, "These narrations explain the meaning of the statement of Allaah . ﴾ **You Muslims are the best of peoples ever raised up for mankind; you enjoin the good and forbid wrongdoing, and you believe in Allaah.** ﴿*

So those people who are rightly characterized by these characteristics, then they enter into those mentioned with these praises for them, and this commendation for them. Just as Qatadah mentioned, "We were informed that 'Umar Ibn al-Khattab, may Allaah be pleased with him, while making his Hajj saw the people proceeding quickly, and so recited this verse . ﴾

You Muslims are the best of peoples ever raised up for mankind ◈ *then he said: 'The one who is pleased to be from this Ummah, then he is included in the characteristics placed by Allaah within it." This was narrated by Ibn Jareer."* Then Ibn Katheer stated, *"And the one who does not truly reflect this description then he resembles the people of the Book as Allaah says,* ◈ *They did not forbid one another from the wrong which they committed. Vile indeed was what they used to do.* ◈-(Surah al-Ma'idah: 79).

So I say: enjoining the good and forbidding wrong is an obligation which has been prescribed upon the Ummah collectively, yet it is not permissible for anyone to abandon what he is individually capable of from fulfilling it. As turning away from such a matter that you are capable of fulfilling inevitably and surely only results in you earning a sin. As the Messenger of Allaah, may Allaah's praise and salutations be upon him, said: *{Enjoin the good and forbid wrongdoing, before you make demands but the people do not respond to you.}*. This was narrated by Ibn Maajah, and it was declared authentic by Imaam al-Albaanee. Additionally, it is reported from Abu Sa'eed, may Allaah be pleased with him that the Prophet, may Allaah's praise and salutations be upon him said, *{ The Prophet said, "Beware! Avoid sitting on the streets." The people said, "There is no other option as these are our only sitting places where we can talk." The Prophet said, "If you must sit there, then observe the rights of the street." They asked, "What are the rights of the street?" He said, "They are the lowering of your gazes, refraining from harming people, returning greetings, and enjoining good and forbidding evil. }* It was narrated by both Imaam al-Bukhaaree and Imaam Muslim in their 'Saheeh' collections.

It is from these evidences found within the Book of Allaah, the Sunnah, and the Consensus of the Muslims which indicate the obligation of enjoining the good and forbidding wrongdoing that we derive the proof of the obligation of refuting that which conflicts with the truth. And refutation is not used except in regard to recognized mistakes. Therefore, is it permissible for us to remain silent regarding such mistakes and errors, and to not forbid them? The answer is: No, and those who forbid the use of refutations to clarify, certainly only desire that, that wrongdoing be allowed to spread without it being opposed. But when matters that are wrong are allowed to spread without being opposed, it causes the strength of falsehood and its people to increase and become more intense, while weakening the position of the truth and the people who adhere to it. Such that if the Earth becomes empty of those enjoining the good and forbidding wrongdoing this is a cause for its people to deserve being cursed, just as occurred with the people of Banee Isra'eel.

Allaah the Most High said, ◈ *Those among the Children of Israel who disbelieved were cursed by the tongue of Dawood and 'Isaa son of Maryam. That was because they disobeyed Allaah and the Messengers and were ever transgressing beyond bounds. They used not to forbid one another from the wrongdoing which they committed. Vile indeed was that which they used to do.* ◈ -(Surah al-Ma'idah: 78-79).

Allaah, the Most High the Most Exalted, has made the excellent status of this Ummah based upon three foundations, they are:

1) enjoining the good

2) forbidding wrongdoing

3) having faith in Allaah

In summary, the one who rejects the use of refutations, is indeed prohibiting the enjoining of good and the forbidding of wrongdoing. And the one who forbids the enjoining of good and the forbidding of wrongdoing has destroyed two of these mentioned three foundations. And if you destroy these two from them, then in fact you have also destroyed the third one from among them- that being faith in

Allaah. Because faith in Allaah is the reason and cause for the enjoining of good and the forbidding of wrongdoing. And through the loss of these two foundations, the people themselves become lost and misguided as Allaah, the Most High has said, *If only there had been among the generations before you, people having wisdom, prohibiting others from all kinds of crimes and sins in the earth, except a few of those whom We saved from among them. Those who did wrong pursued the enjoyment of good things of this worldly life, and were criminals and sinners.* -(Surah Hud: 119) May Allaah's praise and salutations be upon our Prophet Muhammad, his household, and his Companions.

Written by Ahmad Ibn Yahya Ibn Muhammad an-Najmee
5/2/1427

(5)

CLARIFICATION FROM SHEIKH SAALEH AL-
FAUZAAN REGARDING THE FALSEHOOD OF
THOSE WHO STATE THAT WE SHOULD NOT
DECLARE THE ONE WHO OPPOSES THE TRUTH
AS MISTAKEN OR WRONG

All praise is due to Allaah Lord of all the Worlds, praise and salutations be upon our Prophet Muhammad, upon his household, and his Companions. As for what follows:

Currently we find that it is mentioned on the tongues of many writers that it is impermissible to declare the one who opposes the truth as mistaken or wrong, and that it is obligatory that we respect the differing opinions of others, and that it is not permissible to state definitively that what is correct is that which is held by one party or individual as opposed to someone else. But this statement cannot be accepted as true in a general sense. Because what is required by this, is that we consider all those who have opposed the people of the Sunnah and the Jama'ah- as being in some way correct, and as such is would not be permissible that we declare them as mistaken or wrong. And this is a clear deception and misleading, because it contradicts the statement of the Prophet, may Allaah's praise and salutations be upon him, *{ This Ummah will divide into seventy three sects all of them will enter the Hellfire except for one.' It was said, 'Who are they oh Messenger of Allaah?' He replied, 'Those who are upon what I and my Companions are upon today.}*

What is also required by this claim or statement is that in relation the individual who opposes the clear evidence in an issue, which falls into the realm of independent reasoning, one cannot state that he is mistaken or in error. Meaning that you cannot refute him. And this contradicts the statement of the Prophet, may Allaah's praise and salutations be upon him, *{ If one of you strives to reach the truth through an independent judgment and he is correct then he receives two rewards. And if one of you strives to reach the truth through an independent judgment and he is mistaken he receives a single reward }.* This indicates that of the two parties who arrived at clearly differing conclusions striving to reach the truth – one is indeed mistaken. However he receives a reward for his effort. Yet they still should not be followed in the conclusion he reached; because his derived conclusion conflicts with stronger evidences.

As for what is considered correct from this statement, of claiming of that you should not definitively state that one of the differing positions in a matter is mistaken; then this only applies to those issues of independent reasoning in which it is not been made clear that the evidence supports one of the scholars from among those who hold these differing opinions. This is what is expressed in their phrase, "*There is no blame to be directed towards someone in matter solely based upon independent reasoning.*" And "*A judgment reached solely from independent reasoning cannot invalidate another similar judgment.*" Additionally, this is in regard to the people who are specialists in this branch of knowledge from among the scholars, not in relation to the 'intellectuals' and 'thinkers' who do not possess the specialized knowledge to comprehend the proper realm of using independent reasoning, nor the principles that must be used in deriving rulings from the source texts of Islaam, such that they might correctly speak and write regarding these matters.

Moreover, if it was not permissible to declare anyone from the various people who put forth various statements and claims, or those scholars who adhere to specific schools of jurisprudence -wrong or in error, then all of the books of the past, meaning books of refutation and clarification of contradictions to the truth in which the scholars have put forth refutations against those opposers to the truth who brought forth these false claims, then all of these efforts would have to be considered forbidden and rejected by us. Similarly, in relation to the saying of Allaah the Exalted, ❴ *And if you differ in anything amongst yourselves, refer it to Allaah and His Messenger* ❵ -(Surah an-Nisa': 59) what would be its benefit if it has no true significance due to this claim that it is impermissible to declare the one who opposes the truth to be mistaken or wrong? Therefore this restriction is false, and the one makes use of it relies upon falsehood. And we do not hear or read about those who accuse the scholars who refutes those who have opposed various aspects of the truth that they have monopolized what is correct to themselves, and declared as wrong those who have contradicted them, and that they have censured other opinions and thoughts.. until the end of their claims. And this is a false accusation. As those who are considered reliable scholars do not attempt to monopolize what is correct in their statements, rather they declare as wrong those who contradict the affirmed evidences, and look at the heart of the reality of the matter in question. Therefore they refute the one who possesses this characteristics, acting upon the statement of the Prophet, may Allaah's praise and salutations be upon him, *{ The religion is giving advice. It was said, 'To whom?' He replied, For Allaah, His Book, His Messenger, and to the leaders of the Muslims and their general people.}*

Indeed Allaah, the Most Perfect and the Most High, brings forth refutations against the people of falsehood in many places within the Noble Qur'an, and has legislated that we refute them, in order to affirm and bring out the realization of the truth and that exert pressure against and contain falsehood If this was not undertaken then falsehood would spread throughout the earth, and truth would be weakened, such that what is good then becomes something bad, and what is bad becomes something considered good.

Allaah has actually legislated for us that which is more significant than this, and that is jihaad against the people of falsehood with both sword and speech, by proofs and evidences. Allaah the Most High said: *Oh Prophet! Strive hard against the disbelievers and the hypocrites...* -(Surah at-Tahreem: 9) If there occurs from some of those who teach examples of bad manners in their dealing with the people who have opposed aspects of the Book and the Sunnah, which have exceeds the boundaries of the Sharee'ah legislated for refutations, then this is firstly should not to be attributed to the scholars in general, nor should be taken as a proof that we should remain silent from clarifying the truth of a matter, or cease refuting those who have differed with the evidences of Islaam. This is the main point that I wished to warn against, and ◈ *I only desire reform so far as I am able, to the best of my power. And my guidance cannot come except from Allaah, in Him I trust and unto Him I repent.* ◈ -(Surah Hud: 88) Peace and salutations be upon our Prophet Muhammad, upon his household, and his Companions.

[Source: al-Jazeerah magazine: Issue 11672, Yawn al-Ahad, Rajab 27, 1425]

Similarly our sheikh has also stated in '*A Valued Gift for the Reader Of Comments Upon the Book Sharh as-Sunnah*' pages 113-115:

"Imaam Al-Barbahaaree said: '**It is duty for the one who is aware of the condition of the person upon error, to warn the people from him, and to make clear to the people his condition, such that no one falls into his innovation, and then becomes ruined.**'

Explanation: "This is in relation to the one who contradicts the truth knowingly, so it is not permissible to remain silent regarding him. Rather, it is an obligation to expose his condition, uncover his disgraceful distance from the truth, such that the people are warned about him. One should not say, "*The people are free to hold their own opinions, they enjoy freedom of speech, and mutually acknowledge each other's differing opinions!*" As is repeatedly stressed and emphasized these days from the call for mutual respect for differing views. But the issue is not an issue of simply differing opinions, the issue is that of adherence to the way of guidance. Indeed Allaah has delineated for us the single clear path, and said for us to proceed upon it when He said ❴ *And verily, this is my Straight Path, so follow it* ❵ -(Surah al-An'am: 153). Such that if anyone comes to us with a call that indicates that what he desires from us is that we turn away from this clear path, then first of all we reject his speech, and secondly we explain his state and warn the people from him. It is not possible that we should remain silent about him. Because if we were to be silent regarding him, the people will be deceived by him, especially if he is someone who is eloquent in speech or writing, or has pleasing cultivated manners. Then the people would likely be misled by him, saying about him "*This is a worthy individual, this is one of our intellectuals.*". This is a matter known to occur frequently these days. Therefore this is very dangerous matter.

As such, in this situation, it is obligatory to refute the one who opposes the truth, as opposed to the claim of those who say, "*Abandon refutations and just call the people, everybody has his opinion so respect this, and we all have freedom of thought, and freedom of speech...*" and so on. Through this way of theirs the Muslim Ummah will be destroyed. The first righteous generations did not remain silent regarding people like those we have mentioned. Rather they exposed them and refuted them due to their understanding of the danger of these people to the Ummah. As such we cannot proceed to simply remain silent about their evil. Rather, it is required that we clarify what Allaah has revealed of the truth, otherwise we will stand as those who have concealed the truth, from those whom Allaah said about them, ❴ *Verily, those who conceal the clear proofs, evidences and the guidance, which We have sent down, after We have made it clear for the people in the Book, they are the ones cursed by Allaah and cursed by the cursers.* ❵ -(Surah al-Baqarah: 159).

Additionally this affair is not restricted only to innovators in the religion. Rather it encompasses those who remain silent about such innovators, it also includes censuring and criticizing such people. Because it is obligatory to explain and clarify these matters to the people, and this is the function served by knowledge based refutations available in the bookstores of the Muslims. These works of refutation defend the straight path and warn against the like of such misguided individuals as were mentioned. So no one attempts to spread among us this ideological concept- that of absolute freedom of opinion and speech, and mutual respect of every opinion- except for the misguided one who is striving to conceal the truth.

Our goal is only the truth, not merely criticizing others, or simply speaking badly about the people, the goal is the clarification of the what is indeed the truth. And this is the trust and duty which Allaah has laid upon the scholars. Such that silence is not permissible regarding individuals such as we have mentioned. But with great regret, if a scholar comes and refutes the like of such individuals, some people say "*This is recklessness!*" and other statements like this of deceptive whispers. But the people of knowledge have never failed to continue clarifying to the people the evil of misguided individuals, those who are callers to falsehood, they have never ceased doing so."

(6)

CLARIFICATION FROM THE SHEIKH
MUHAMMAD NAASIRUDDEEN AL-ALBAANEE,
MAY ALLAAH HAVE MERCY UPON HIM,
REGARDING THE ROLE &
PLACE OF HARSHNESS

The sheikh, may Allaah have mercy upon him said in his introduction to *'Silsilat al-Ahaadeeth ad-Dha'eefah'* page 27:

"In closing this introduction, it is necessary that I direct a statement to every sincere individual from among the readers of this work, those who have love towards me or as well as those who have some hatred. So I say: Often some people ask me concerning the reason for my harshness, which at times appears in some of my writings when refuting some of the writers who oppose or contradict me. In response to this I say:

Those readers should know that I, and all praise is due to Allaah, do not take this way with anyone who refutes me with a refutation that is based upon knowledge, nor do I attack him. In fact, I stand in regard to him as one who is thankful. So if there is some aspect of harshness in any place within my writings, then this returns to either one of the following two situations.

As for the first situation, it is to be found in my response to one who has himself originally sought to refute me, but gone beyond the proper bounds and oppressed me to an astonishing level with defamation and slander. Such as Abu Ghuddah for example, or al-Adhamee who hides behind the name "Salafee Guide"! Or those like Ghumaaree, al-Bootee, or others. Or such as Sheikh Ismaa'eel al-'Ansaaree as occurred on more than one occasion, and this is after a significant time has passed!

As well as directing this towards the likes of those oppressors who in my belief will not benefit from my acting towards them with pardon and gentleness. Rather, that way in fact only harms them and encourages them to continue further in their injustice and enmity. Just as a poet has stated:

If you treat the noble person well you gain some mastery over him,

> *But if you treat a wicked person nobly he only rebels further.*

As using generosity in the place where the sword belongs only brings harm,

> *Just as using the sword harms, in the instance in which generosity is required.*

Indeed, I am able to endure the oppression from those who would bring that forth, if it is in order to guide and teach the people. Yet it may sometimes reach a level that is above ones human capacity to tolerate. Due to this, the Islamic Sharee'ah comes with that which conforms to that level of human capacity. Moreover we do not say, all praise is due to Allaah, as is found in that book which they claim today is the Injeel, "*The one who strikes you upon your right cheek, then offer to him your left. And the one who takes your lower garment, then willingly give him your upper garment*"!

Rather Allaah the Exalted says, …Then whoever transgresses the prohibition against you, you transgress likewise against him… -(Surah al-Baqarah: 194) and He said, The recompense for an evil is an evil like thereof -(Surah ash-Shuraa: 40) And I say that from the blessings of Allaah is that He has completed what is partially stated in this verse in another verse, "…but whoever forgives and makes reconciliation, his reward is due from Allaah. Verily, He likes not the oppressors, and wrong-doers" and And verily, whosoever shows patience and forgives that would truly be from the things recommended by Allaah. -(Surah ash-Shuraa: 40-43).

However, I do believe that pardoning is commendable, and patience is something one is rewarded for; yet this is only in relation to those who you have the general belief that it will benefit that oppressor and not harm him further, and will elevate the one who patiently endured the oppression and not humiliate him. As this is shown in the practical examples from life history of The Messenger, may Allaah's praise and salutations be upon him, in his dealing with those who opposed him. As he, may Allaah's praise and salutations be upon him, said, {The most severely punished person on the Day of Judgment is the man who killed a prophet of Allaah.}

The very least that can be taken from these and similar verses is that it is permitted for the one who has been oppressed to stand up for himself using the truth without him then being considered from among those who has also committed oppression. Such as the statement of Allaah,

Allaah does not like that the evil should be uttered in public except by him who has been wronged... -(Surah an-Nisa': 148.) And the Sunnah affirms this and clarifies it. Such as his statement, may Allaah's praise and salutations be upon him, to 'Aisha when one of her fellow wives treated her badly. He said, {Please, take your retribution.} 'Aisha said, "So I responded to her until I saw that her mouth was dried out, and she could not respond or return a single word back to me. Then I saw that the face of the Prophet, was shining and radiant."

Therefore I hope those readers are not quick to blame me, as I have been oppressed by many who stand forth as claimants to knowledge, and some of them were those who I had thought stood with us upon the path of the first generations of this Ummah. But, if they actually were upon our methodology, then they were from those overtaken by hatred and jealousy within themselves. As is mentioned in the narration, { The diseases found in the previous nations will creep into your hearts, such as jealousy and hatred. And indeed it does not shave away hair, it shaves away the religion itself. } This is an authentic narration due to its many various chains of narration from both the Companions Ibn Zubayr and Abu Hurairah.

Additionally, I would hope that those who are asking this question would be those who possess a good grasp of our actual situation, and do not hold a perception that is imaginary and impractical. And that they find acceptable from me that I have stopped in my responses to these oppressors at a point which is in accordance with the statement of the Lord of all the worlds, ...and transgress not. Verily, Allaah does not like the transgressors. -(Surah al-Ma'idah: 87) without responding to that in a way which reflects the old ways of the Days of Ignorance, the period before Islaam:

It is hoped that no one enters into acting ignorantly with us,
   For fear that our own ignorance might rise against those
   who acted towards us so.

And I seek refuge in Allaah from being among those who are ignorant.

As for the second situation, it is when there is a shocking and momentous error in relation to a hadeeth of the Messenger of Allaah, may Allaah's praise and salutations be upon him, originating from those who are known to not verify matters sufficiently. Therefore I may proceed harshly against such an individual in my speech against him, due to my vigilance and concern for the hadeeth of the Messenger of Allaah, may Allaah's praise and salutations be upon him. Such as the following statements of mine, regarding hadeeth number 142:

"*Why is Suyootee not ashamed- may Allaah pardon us and him- to use this false chain of narration as a support to strengthen the other chain of narration. As the narrator (Abu Dunya) is known as a liar and fabricator, and this state of his is not hidden from as-Suyutee...*"

So what has lead to this type of harshness is my vigilance and concern for the hadeeth of the Messenger of Allaah, may Allaah's praise and salutations be upon him. Because something is being attributed to him which he in fact did not say. And we have been preceded in this by some of the scholars who were from the preservers of hadeeth narrations who were well known for their steadfastness in the religion and the fear of Allaah within their actions. Look, for example, at the statement of Imaam ad-Dhahabee, may Allaah have mercy upon him, regarding the ruling of Haakim; when he, Haakim had authenticated a narration regarding the merits of 'Alee Ibn Abee Taalib, may Allaah be pleased with him- number 757:

"*I say, rather it is fabricated, and its narrator Ahmad al-Haraanee is a fabricator of hadeeth. So how can such ignorance come from someone of your great understanding?!*"

Therefore the reader should carefully study and consider to see if there is any difference between the two scholars Haakim and as-Suyootee on one hand, and between the expression used by Imaam ad-Dhahabee in regard to Haakim, and my expression regarding Suyootee on the other hand."

(7)

CLARIFICATION FROM SHEIKH MUHAMMAD
IBN SAALEH AL-'UTHEIMEEN, MAY ALLAAH
HAVE MERCY UPON HIM, REGARDING VARIOUS
CONCEPTS AND PRINCIPLES THAT CONFLICT
WITH THE WAY OF THE SALAF.

The following are a number of questions and answers from Sheikh al-'Utheimeen, may Allaah have mercy upon him, from a transcript transmitted by Sheikh Rabee'a al-Madkhalee in his book *"A Defense Against the Aggressions of Adnan Against the Scholars of the Sunnah and al-Emaan"* (beginning on page 23):

Questioner: *"We are a group of students and we want to study that which is the religion of Allaah in truth, meaning that which the Messenger and his Companions stood upon, and that religion which they were followed in by the scholars of the Sunnah and guidance. Yet some matters and issues are doubtful and unclear to us, specifically some matter that have been put forth by modern individuals who have attributed themselves to knowledge. This is especially the case in relation to various fundamentals and principles, such as the following principles. The first of them is:*

'We do not speak about mistakes of the people of innovation in the religion or those who have transmitted the religion, rather one should say: 'Give advice but do not criticize.'"

Sheikh al-'Utheimeen: This is an error, rather we criticize the one who is obstinate in the face of the truth.

Questioner: *Our sheikh, the second principle is that it is said, 'The one who rules upon others, he himself is then ruled upon and judged.'*

Sheikh al-'Utheimeen: Never, this is a principle used to seek favor or support from others.

Questioner: *Our sheikh, the third principle is that it is said, 'There is no connection between one's intention and what one does or how one acts, neither in the beginning of the matter nor from afterwards.'*

Sheikh al-'Utheimeen: This is a lie, because of the statement of the Messenger of Allaah, may Allaah's praise and salutations be upon him, said *{Verily, deeds are by their intentions...}*

Questioner: *Our sheikh, the fourth principle is that it is said, 'It stands as a condition brought forth by some of the people that in the criticism of the people of innovation in the religion and others must be affirm by definitive evidences which there is absolutely no doubt concerning.'*

Sheikh al-'Utheimeen: This is not correct.

Questioner: *Our sheikh, the fifth principle is that it is said, 'It stands as a condition brought forth by some of the people that anyone, meaning a scholar, hears a mistake from someone who has made or fallen into error or innovation in the religion in a book, that he must elaborate the details or that he should give the mistaken individual advice before he rules upon him, before he publically explains and clarifies that mistake or issue of innovation in the religion.'*

Sheikh al-'Utheimeen: This is correct.

Questioner: *However, our sheikh, it is said: 'The one who contradicts this is characterized by one of the characteristics of the hypocrites.'*

Sheikh al-'Utheimeen: That is not true.

Questioner: *Our sheikh, the last principle, the sixth, is that it is said, 'The one who acts justice and fairness in the issue of giving of advice and warning from innovation in the religion and the people of innovation should mention their good deeds along side of their errors or mistakes.'*

Sheikh al-'Utheimeen: I say to you no, no this is an error.

Questioner: *Assuredly, sheikh, and related to this principle it has been said, 'If you mention the merits of the people of the Sunnah, then that is from justice and fairness, that you mention their shortcomings along with their merits and good characteristics.'*

Sheikh al-'Utheimeen: Listen to me, young man, in the situation of refuting it is not suitable that I mention the merits of the individual I am refuting. If I were to mention that individual's merits, while I am refuting him, then this weakens my refutation of his error.

Questioner: *Even when dealing with the people of the Sunnah our sheikh?*

Sheikh al-'Utheimeen: This is in relation to both the people of the Sunnah as well as other than them. As when I am putting forth a refutation, how could it be that I am refuting someone and I start to bring forth his praise and merits? Is this sensible?

The sheikh, may Allaah have mercy upon him, was also asked:

Questioner: *There are some statements that we wish to present to you for you to comment upon sheikh. In order that is can be seen whether the people of the Sunnah and the Jama'ah agree with them. It is said: 'Anyone who investigates the splitting and differences that that have occurred between the various groups that state that they are working for Islaam will find that the majority of them have causes that stem from issues of morals and character, not fundamental issues of correct beliefs or the methodology of Islaam.' So what is your view of this statement?*

Sheikh al-'Utheimeen: This is not true, this is not true. Rather, the issues behind these divisions are fundamental issues of correct beliefs and the methodology of Islaam. The sect of the Khawaarij has a specific methodology, and the sect of the Shee'ah likewise has a specific methodology.

Questioner: *May Allaah grant you steadfastness. It is also said: 'The differences between the various groups are differences of acceptable independent judgment. This is fact that I acknowledge, and likewise due to which I do not easily consider or taken these groups outside of fold of Islaam.' So what is your view of this statement?*

Sheikh al-'Utheimeen: There is no doubt that some of these differences are related to independent judgments, and some of them I see as more significant and serious. Therefore those matters of difference in which the truth is clear and apparent then the one who stands in opposition to it is a stubborn prideful opposer. While in those matters of difference in which it is not evident and obvious from evidence what is correct, then this is what falls into the realm of independent judgment.

Questioner: *May Allaah grant you steadfastness. It is also claimed that: 'If the matter is one of studying a specific individual then it is required that you mention both their merits and the mistakes such that you are able to arrive at a conclusion that you can then work with. This is the way of Imaam ad-Dhahabee and the leading scholars of criticism and commendation in the religion.' So is it true that the scholars of scholars of criticism and commendation in the religion that when they proceeded to mention the state of narrators mentioned both their merits and the mistakes together?*

Sheikh al-'Utheimeen: No, no, look at this and consider, may Allaah bless you. If the case is one where we wish to refute an individual, then we do not mention his merits and good deeds, because this weakens an aspect of that refutation. But if we wish to give an account of their life, such as in a biography, then in this case it is necessary that you mention every aspect of their life's affairs.

Questioner: *May Allaah grant you steadfastness. What is your esteemed view about an individual who advises the youth to read the books of Sayyed Qutb? And specially his books, "In the Shade of the Qur'an", "Milestones upon the path" "Why I have been Executed" without explaining the errors that are present in this books?*

Sheikh al-'Utheimeen: I hold, may Allaah bless you, that if he is truly someone offering guiding advice for Allaah, for His Messenger, to the Muslims, he should encourage the people to read the books of the early generations that explain the meanings of the Qur'an as well as their books in other than this subject. They contain great blessing and benefit and are sounder than the books of the people from the latter generations. As for the explanation of the Qur'an by

Sayyed Qutb, may Allaah have mercy upon him, it contains abominable and grievously false statements. However, we hope Allaah forgive him for that. This explanation of the Qur'an has abominable statements such as his false explanation the meaning of Allaah rising above His Throne, and his false explanation of Surah "Qul huu Allaahu Ahad" -Surah Ikhlaas, and likewise his erroneously describing some of the Messengers of Allaah with descriptions that are not at all proper or fitting for them.

The sheikh, may Allaah have mercy upon him, was also asked:

Questioner: *Here are some questions sheikh that we hope you would allow us to present to you, if Allaah so wills. What is your view of of sheikh, of the following statement, 'After ten years then people have become united, therefore there is no need to study the books teaching correct beliefs such as 'Aqeedah at-Tahaweeyah' and 'Aqeedah al-Wasateeyah' and 'Aqeedah al-Hamaweeyah' and 'Aqeedah al-Tadrumeeyah' or 'Jawharat at-Tawheed'.*

Sheikh al-'Utheimeen: This is something good, that we hope will be, something that we will receive news of this happening.

Questioner: *Yet this means at present, it is stated that after ten years now people have become united, therefore there is no need to study these books which we have mentioned to you.*

Sheikh al-'Utheimeen: I ask you, is this a statement made about something hoping from Allaah that it will occur, hoping that after ten years the people have become united, and that we will receive certain news of this occurring?

Questioner: *By Allaah sheikh, no this means our present state, this statement has already been made. And we do not understand what is intended with this!*

Sheikh al-'Utheimeen: What is important to take note of in this, is that at present, it is indeed required that we study the correct beliefs.

Questioner: *Allaah is great! Yes, yes, this addresses his meaning. So is this statement is incorrect sheikh?*

Sheikh al-'Utheimeen: It is incorrect, because at present the people are in true need of studying this subject, as in what area is the present deviation and misguidance more significant than of the correct beliefs....

The noble sheikh also responded in a separate answer to a questioner who asked:

"Has the sunnah or practice of criticizing and commending individuals in the religion died and ceased? And what is the ruling regarding refuting the one who has contradicted something from the guidance of Islaam due to hating to enter into examining him or looking at him personally."

Sheikh al-'Utheimeen, may Allaah have mercy upon him, answered,

"I fear that this statement is a true word by which falsehood is intended. As all praise is due to Allaah, the practice of criticism and commendation of individuals has not died, nor has it been buried, nor has not become feeble and sick. It is present and established. Indeed the practice of criticism and commendation of individuals is found within the evaluating of those witnesses who testify in front of the judge in court. As perhaps individuals testifying in a case may be questionable or unconfirmed, and so they seek clarifying testimony from them; and it is also used within the area of transmission of reports. Certainly we just listened to the rectification of the imaam of the statement of Allaah, the Most High; ◈ *Oh you who believe! If a rebellious evil person comes to you with a news, verify it* ◈ -(Surah Al-Hujuraat: 6)

Consequently, the practice of criticizing and commending individuals remains present as long as individuals of different types of acceptability will be found, as long as individuals of different levels of reliability will be found- the practice of criticizing and commending individuals will remain.

However, I fear that someone might say for instance that "*This specific individual has been criticized.*" When he has not in fact been criticized. Such that they will take this apparent ruling as a means to spread and attribute faults to the people. For this reason I say. If an individual has a specific fault and there is a need for, a demand for, or it is seen that the overall benefit lies in clarifying his fault specifically and particularly; then there is no harm in this, certainly there is no harm in doing this. However, it is better that one would say: "*Some people have done such and such criticized action*" or "*Some people have said such and such criticized statement*". And this is for two reasons:

The first reasons is it is free from the issues related to specifying someone particularly.

And the second reason is that then the clarification is a general judgement upon him as well as others who are similar to him.

With the exception of the case when we see that a specific person has caused trials among the people, and he calls to innovation, and invites towards misguidance, then in this case it is required that we specifically identify him, in order that the people are not deceived by him."

[Source audio file in the voice of Sheikh Muhammad Ibn Saaleh al-'Utheimeen]

(8)

CLARIFICATIONS FROM SHEIKH SAALEH
FAUZAAN REGARDING BOOKS OF REFUTATION
AND THEIR EFFECT UPON CALLING TO ALLAAH.
& REGARDING THE FINAL POSITION OF THE
GUIDING SCHOLAR SHEIKH 'ABDUL-'AZEEZ IBN
BAAZ, MAY ALLAAH HAVE MERCY UPON HIM
TOWARDS THE GROUP JAMA'AT AT-TABLEEGH

Sheikh Fauzaan, may Allaah preserve him, said in his work entitled, *"Beneficial Answers to Questions on New Methodologies"*: page 9

Question: What is your view of the book 'al-Qutubiyyah'? Do you advise that it should be read, and are such books of refutation from the methodology of the first three righteous generations of Muslims (may Allaah have mercy upon them)?

Answer: The refutation of the one who differs from the truth is from the practice and way of the first three generations. Those of the first generations refuted those who opposed the truth, and their books containing these refutations are present and available. Imaam Ahmad refuted the corrupters who left he religion due to their beliefs and those Muslims who innovated in the religion. Sheikh al-Islaam Ibn Taymeeyah refuted the people of theoretical philosophy, the scholars of false rhetorical concepts, the people of the innovation of Sufism, and those who worshiped at graves. Additionally, Imaam Ibn Qayyim, as well as many of the leading scholars, refuted those people who opposed the truth in order to explain the truth and make it apparent to the people; in order that the Muslim nation not be lead astray and follow the people of error and those who had opposed the truth. This is from advising the Muslim Ummah.

As for the Book *"al-Qutbeeyah"* as well as other books, if what it contains is correct and true, then we must accept it. If those who composed the refutation of the one who opposed the truth accurately transmitted from that individual's statements found in his books and from his recorded lectures, mentioning the name of the book or cassette containing the false statements by page number and volume, and the statements which he brings forth are clearly in error, then what would prevent the one who brings forth a refutation of the one in error?!? The purpose is sincerely advising the people, not disparaging or criticizing individuals. Indeed the intent is advising the people and clarifying matters to them. As such the book *"al-Qutbeeyah"* or similar works do not bring forth lies against anyone, but simply transmit from the statements of those who have opposed the truth, not transmitting it by meaning only, or in a summarized form which distorts. Instead, they transmit it with the full text and specify the volume in which it is found and the page where it was found- indeed, even stating the line number where the statement was made. So what is wrong with this?! As for those of us who are silent regarding the errors of people, we are deceived by the people. Therefore, we say: These books which are commonly found in the hands of the youth and with general people- they contain concealed poisons as well as errors. They deceive the Muslim nation, and it is not permissible. It is necessary that it be explained and clarified, and that advice is given. It is necessary the good be enjoined and wrongdoing forbidden. These books of refutation have been present among us from the ages long past and no one found fault or discredited them, as all praise is due to Allaah, it is necessary to explain and clarify affairs.

Sheikh Fauzaan, may Allaah preserve him, said in work entitled, *"Beneficial Answers to Questions on New Methodologies"*: page 148

Question: Is explaining and clarifying some of the errors found in the books of the people of division and partisanship or of the numerous groups coming to our land considered to be harmful to the efforts to call to Allaah?

Answer: No, this is not considered harmful to the call to the truth and inviting to Islaam, because these books are not truly books calling to the truth and Islaam. Additionally these individuals, the authors of these books and concepts, are not from those who call to Islaam with insight into matters, with sound knowledge, and upon the truth. So when we explain the mistakes found within these books, or the mistakes of these individuals, it is not to be considered simply personal criticism. Instead, it should be considered from the aspect of advising the Ummah of that harm which is entering into it in the form of dubious concepts, which will eventually become a trial for us, and cause the loss of our united word and stance, and lead to divisions within our united ranks. So our objective is not the criticism of individuals. Our objective is the criticism of those false and deficient concepts and understandings found in the books brought among us in the name of calling to Islaam.

Sheikh Fauzaan, may Allaah preserve him, said in his commentary entitled, "*A Valued Gift for the Reader: Comments upon the Book Sharh as-Sunnah*": page 230-232:

"… '*So do not proceed along with him upon his path or methodology*', meaning because he will have an effect upon you, and draw you into his way of innovation. Especially if you have a good opinion of him, due to what he reflects of diligence in worship, austerity, and distance from worldly pleasures. As these matters will obscure and screen from you his innovation in the religion; and this is something extremely dangerous. This is just like the example which the Prophet put forward for us of the righteous sitting companion being like a seller of musk- either he will give you some of his musk as a gift, or you may purchase some from him, or you simply enjoy from him the excellent smell while you continue to sit with him. Such that even if you do not receive anything from him either as a present or as a purchase, then still there is that excellent smell which you experience while sitting with him. But as for the evil sitting companion, then his example is said to be like the blacksmith- either some spark coming from his work will burn your clothing, or at the very least you will experience from him an awful smell.

This example applies and holds true for the group Jama'at at-Tableegh by whom many of the people today are deceived and beguiled through what is observed from them of acts of worship and turning away from sins as is said, and the strong affect they have upon those who spend some time with and accompany them. But this group takes the one who commits sins away from that sin and leads him into innovation in the religion! As innovation in the religion is worse and more evil than sinning. The individual who only commits sins from among the people of the Sunnah, is better than the devoted worshiper from the people who have altered and innovated matters within the religion.

So you should take heed of this. And I do not say this due to any aversion to the good that they possess, as they do possess some good. But indeed I say this because of hating innovation in the religion, as indeed innovation causes ones good to pass away.

The innovation which is found within Jama'at at-Tableegh has been stated clearly by those who used to be part of this group but then repented from their association and participation with them. These individuals have written several books warning from them and clarifying and explaining the innovation of their path.

Sheikh Muhammad Ibn Ibraaheem, the former Muftee of the Kingdom, initially allowed some of them to engage in their efforts of "calling" in the kingdom of Saudi Arabia, as their true state was not clear to him. But later, once the nature of their way became apparent to him, he put forth a refutation against them that was a strong refutation, as is found in his compilation of rulings. He had made it a condition upon them that they call to the worship of Allaah alone, but they did not fulfill this condition. Similarly, Sheikh Ibn Baaz initially praised them, because their true state was not clear to him. And when their actual state was clarified to him, he retracted that initial praise saying, "*You should not go out with them, except for the one who wishes to call them to the truth and the reality of Allaah's right of being worshipped without partners, and in order to criticize them for what practices they engage in which contradict the Book and the Sunnah.*" That is what he said, may Allaah have mercy upon him. So this understanding of when it is permissible to sit with them stands along with the general reality that the one firmly upon innovation does not usually accept the call to reject and turn away from his innovation. Similarly, the one firmly upon a newly devised methodology does not usually abandon or leave his adopted methodology, for which he may have taken an oath of allegiance to some sheikh.

'As you are not safe from finding his methodology pleasing, and so end up destroyed in your religion along with him', This is the inevitable result if you proceed along with him, and sit with him- that his way will be made pleasing to you. He may conceal from you his innovation, such that later you eventually approve of it and so fall into destruction in your religion along with him. As then you have become someone who has innovated in the religion. Therefore it can be clearly seen the extreme danger of mixing with those who have innovated in the religion, and indeed how many of them are there in this age!

Yet it is also an obligation that we understand what is truly an innovation, as some of the people consider every matter something of innovation. But what is considered innovation is something that is determined through specific guidelines. And as such, if you do verify and confirm that what an individual proceeds upon is innovation in the religion, then do not sit with him and do not be a companion of his."

A Brief Summary & Review

Alhamdulillah, the words of the noble scholars presented here and in various other works and articles remove and clarify many of the doubts regarding their scholastic efforts to protect the Muslims from misguidance and preserve Islaam through refutations and clarifications of mistakes. Any Muslim who truly judges by the Book of Allaah and the Sunnah of the Messenger of Allaah, and is guided by the statements and practice of the guiding leading scholars found in every age should affirm the necessity of clarifying that which opposes the guidance of the Book and the Sunnah and indicating those who openly call to anything which opposed the guidance of the Book of Allaah and the Sunnah. Every striving sincere Muslim should affirm and acknowledge that:

1. It is a necessary aspect of calling to the worship of Allaah alone.

As Sheikh Muhammad Ibn Ramzaan al-Haajaree, may Allaah preserve him, answered the followed question in an open meeting recorded on the Jumaada ath-Thaanee 28, 1432, moderated by Sheikh Abu Bakr La'weesee:

Question: It says here- There are those who say that in our age it is obligatory to only clarify to the people the matter of tawheed, or the right of Allaah to be worshiped alone without any associate, not that we also be concerned with clarifying matters of innovation and newly brought forth matters in the religion, nor that we concern ourselves with refutations against the people of innovation in the religion. So what is your response to this misunderstanding? May Allaah preserve you and bless your affair.

Sheikh al-Haajaree, replied: *This way of both affairs is the very call of Muhammad, may the praise and salutations of Allaah be upon him. He used to say, {**Oh people, say there is none worthy or worship other than Allaah, and you will be successful.**} Yet he would also say in every juma'ah khutbah, {**The most truthful speech is the speech of Allaah, and the best of guidance is the guidance of Muhammad (may the praise and salutations of Allaah be upon him), and every invented matter in the religion in an innovation, and every innovation is a misguidance, and every misguidance is in the Hellfire.**} So his call was comprehensive, being established upon both calling to the worship of Allaah alone, and warning against any innovation in the religion."*

Additionally Sheikh Saaleh al-Fauzaan, mentions,

*"...As such, in this situation, it is obligatory to refute the one who opposes the truth, as opposed to the claim of those who say, "**Abandon refutations and just call the people. Everybody has his opinion so respect this, and we all have freedom of thought, and freedom of speech...**" and so on. Through this way of theirs the Muslim Ummah will be destroyed. The first righteous generations did not remain silent regarding people like those we have mentioned. Rather they exposed them and refuted them due to their understanding of the danger of these people to the Ummah. As such we cannot proceed to simply remain silent about their evil."* [1]

Similarly Sheikh Muhammad Ibn Sa'eed Raslaan further emphasizes this point, in a juma'ah khutbah entitled, *"The Principles of Our Call"*

"...And one of these matters is not correctly established without the other. So the one who calls, to adherence to the Sunnah and worship of Allaah alone, but does not warn against innovation in the religion, has done something

---

[1] A Valued Gift for the Reader Of Comments Upon the Book Sharh as-Sunnah' pages 113-115

wrong, fallen short, and acted one-sidedly. As the Prophet, may the praise and salutations of Allaah be upon him and his household, explained this, as is found in the hadeeth of Irbaadh Ibn Saareeah, may Allaah the Most High be pleased with him.

*He, may the praise and salutations of Allaah be upon him and his household, said. { **And whoever lives for some time amongst you will see tremendous differing, so stick to what you know from my Sunnah and the sunnah of my rightly guided successors. Cling to that with your molar teeth....}** But he did not consider sufficient only this command to adhere to the Sunnah, rather he followed it by warning against innovation in the religion. As he, may the praise and salutations of Allaah be upon him and his household, continued on to say: {...**and beware of newly invented matters, as every newly invented matter in innovation, and every innovation is misguidance.}***

Therefore there must be both the commanding to adhere to the Sunnah, and there must be warning against innovation in the religion. As such, along with commanding others to adhere to the Sunnah, there must also be warning against innovation; there must also be warning against innovation in the religion and its people."

2. It is a practice which has never ceased among the Muslims and will continue until the Day of Judgement.

The Imaam Sheikh Muhammad Ibn Saaleh al-'Utheimen, may Allaah have mercy upon him, stated about this doubt,

"As all praise is due to Allaah, the practice of criticism and commendation of individuals has not died, nor has it been buried, nor has it become feeble and sick. It is present and established....

...Consequently, the practice of criticizing and commending individuals remains present as long as individuals of different types of acceptability will be found, as long as individuals of different levels of reliability will be found- the practice of criticizing and commending individuals will remain." [2]

Likewise the noble Sheikh Rabee'a Ibn Haadee, may Allaah preserve him, stated,

"As for their statement that the period of criticism and commendation has ended, then this is a lie and a deception. The methodology within Islaam of criticizing that which conflicts with the truth will never end until the Day of Judgment begins. The implementation of the way of criticism and commendation in the religion will never cease until the Day of Judgment. There will always be present among us innovation in the religion as well as clear hallmarks and examples of misguidance. Consequently there will always be callers to and leaders of that misguidance up until the Day of Judgment. So likewise there will always remain the need to strive against them, and certainly this is superior to military struggle against ones enemies....

Therefore the struggle always continues between the truth and falsehood, between guidance and misguidance, between the people of the truth and the people of falsehood, and between the people of guidance and the people of misguidance. And as such it is required that the swords of critical examination and criticism and commendation be unsheathed against the people of falsehood..." [3]

---

[2]   Source Audio file in the voice of Sheikh Muhammad Ibn Saaleh al-'Utheimeen

[3]   The Answers of the Esteemed Salafee Sheikh Rabee'a Ibn Haadee al-Madkhalee to the Questions related to Methodology from Abu Rawaahah

3. It is enjoining the good and forbidding evil.

As is mentioned by Sheikh Ahmad an-Najmee, may Allaah have mercy upon him, in a letter dated 5/2/1427

> "...And in reality, refuting the one who has differed with the Book and the Sunnah is considered an aspect of forbidding wrongdoing which is outward and apparent, and refuting falsehoods that are being promoted among the people. Moreover Allaah has joined this matter of enjoining the good and forbidding wrongdoing with one's faith. And He has made the three of them matters leading to the well being of the Ummah. ﴾**You Muslims are the best of peoples ever raised up for mankind; you enjoin the good and forbid wrongdoing, and you believe in Allaah.**﴿ -(Surah Aal-'Imraan: 110)...
>
> ...It is from these evidences found within the Book of Allaah, the Sunnah, and the Consensus of the Muslims which indicate the obligation of enjoining the good and forbidding wrongdoing that we derive the proof of the obligation of refuting that which conflicts with the truth. And refutation is not used except in regard to recognized mistakes."

And Sheikh Ibn Baaz, may Allaah have mercy upon him, mentioned,

> "However, the obligation to unite the Muslims and join their voices together upon the truth, and to hold fast to the rope of Allaah, does not require the abandoning of forbidding wrongdoing whether from actions or beliefs of the followers of Sufism or others. Rather, doing so is itself a requirement of the command to hold fast to the rope of Allaah and to enjoin good and forbid wrongdoing, and to make clear the truth for the one who has strayed from it, or who believes something which opposes the truth with evidences from the Sharee'ah until we are united upon the truth and have rejected that which opposes it.

This is a requirement of the statement of Allaah, ❖*Help you one another in goodness and piety but do not help one another in sin and transgression.*❖*-(Surah al-Maidah:2) and the statement of Allaah, the Most Perfect :*❖*Let there arise out of you a group of people inviting to all that is good (Islaam), enjoining every matter of good and forbidding every matter of wrongdoing and evil. And it is they who are the successful.*❖*-(Surah Aal-'Imraan:104). When the people of truth are silent and refrain from explaining mistakes of those who have made them, and the errors of those who have fallen into them, then they have not fulfilled that which Allaah has commanded them from calling to good and enjoining what is right and forbidding wrongdoing."* [4]

4. It is offering sincere advice to the Muslims.

As is mentioned by Sheikh Saaleh al-Fauzaan,

"...So when we explain the mistakes found within these books, or the mistakes of these individuals, it is not to be considered simply personal criticism. Instead, it should be considered from the aspect of advising the Ummah of that harm which is entering into it in the form of dubious concepts, which will eventually become a trial for us, and cause the loss of our united word and stance, and lead to divisions within our united ranks. So our objective is not the criticism of individuals. Our objective is the criticism of those false and deficient concepts and understandings found in the books brought among us in the name of calling to Islaam." [5]

There is also found within another of his statements,

---

[4]   A Collection of Rulings and Various Statements': Vol. 3, Page 68
[5]   Beneficial Answers to Questions on New Methodologies': Page 148

"....If those who composed the refutation of the one who opposed the truth accurately transmitted from that individual's statements found in his books and from his recorded lectures, mentioning the name of the book or cassette containing the false statements by page number and volume, and the statements which he brings forth are clearly in error, then what legitimate reasons would prevent the one who brings forth a refutation of the one in error from doing so?!?

As the purpose is sincerely advising the people, not disparaging or criticizing individuals. Indeed the intent is advising the people and clarifying matters to them." [6]

5. It is a practice which brings forth required clarifications of the religion, not mere attacks upon people and speaking badly about others.

As is mentioned by Sheikh Saaleh al-Fauzaan,

"Our goal is only the truth, not merely criticizing others, or simply speaking badly about the people. The goal is the clarification of the what is indeed the truth. And this is the trust and duty which Allaah has laid upon the scholars.

...the people of knowledge have never failed to continue clarifying to the people the evil of misguided individuals, those who are callers to falsehood; they have never ceased doing so." [7]

As Sheikh Muhammad Ibn Ramzaan al-Haajaree, may Allaah preserve him said:

"Secondly: Refuting the people of innovation in the religion and warning from them is a foundation from the

[6]   Beneficial Answers to Questions on New Methodologies': Page 9
[7]   A Valued Gift for the Reader Of Comments Upon the Book Sharh as-Sunnah' pages 113-115

foundations of the methodology of those adhering to the way first generations of Muslims.

This is a tremendous foundation from the foundations of the people of the Sunnah, meaning the people of hadeeth and the transmitted narrations who are firmly established upon the religion as it was originally established. And this foundation is nothing other than a means to preserve this religion from deviations and alterations, as a realization of the promise of Allaah, ❁ **Verily we have revealed the dhikr, and we shall preserve it.**" (Surah al-Hajr: 9).

The goal of refutations again the people of innovation and warning against them is not personal revenge or retaliation in order to settle the score in personal disputes that have no connection to the religion, as a group from among the people of biased partisan groups and organizations continually claim in order to misrepresent this matter to the younger generation. This claim is an attempt to defend themselves from the thrusts of refutations from those guiding scholars who have criticized them, and exposed to the Muslim Ummah the reality of their condition which they strive to conceal by wearing an outer garment of soft hearted words, raised enthusiasms, and embellished statements.

Indeed, decisive refutations against the people of desires and innovations have been brought forward continually since the time of the Prophet up until our present time, and will remain until the Day of Judgment. Could the warning of the Prophet against the sect of the Khawaarij, and his mentioning of their characteristics, be considered anything other than an established basis for this foundation of the Salafee methodology?" [8]

---

[8] Clear Expositions of the Differences Between the Call to the way of the First Generations & that of the Innovated Biased Partisian Calls & Movements, pg 256

6. It is the practice of the scholars past and present even though it may contain legitimate harshness.

When the well-known scholars speak harshly against someone who has opposed the guidance of Islaam, it is not from their desires. Rather it is only from their legitimate efforts of defending the truth, as mentioned by Sheikh al-Albaanee, may Allaah have mercy upon him, discussing the situation in which he speaks with some harness in his refutations,

"...As for the second situation, it is when there is a shocking and momentous error in relation to a hadeeth of the Messenger of Allaah, may Allaah's praise and salutations be upon him, originating from those who are known to not verify matters sufficiently. Therefore I may proceed harshly against such an individual in my speech against him, due to my vigilance and concern for the hadeeth of the Messenger of Allaah, may Allaah's praise and salutations be upon him. For example as the following statements of mine, regarding hadeeth number 142:

'Why is as-Suyootee not ashamed- may Allaah pardon us and him- to use this false chain of narration as a support to strengthen the other chain of narration. As the narrator (Abu Dunya) is known as a liar and fabricator, and this state of his is not hidden from as-Suyutee...'

So what has lead to this type of harshness is my vigilance and concern for the hadeeth of the Messenger of Allaah, may Allaah's praise and salutations be upon him. Because something is being attributed to him which he in fact did not say. And we have been preceded in this by some of the scholars who were from the preservers of hadeeth narrations who were well known for their steadfastness in the religion and the fear of Allaah within their actions." [9]

---

[9] 'Silsilat al-Ahaadeeth ad-Dha'eefah' page 27:

This is in regard to legitimate harshness, which the way of the Salaf shows has a role in refutations. Yet even in cases in which incorrect manners are used which the scholars do not approve of, then we must always remember that as Sheikh Saaleh al-Fauzaan, may Allaah preserve him, mentions,

"....If there occurs from some of those who teach examples of bad manners in their dealing with the people who have opposed aspects of the Book and the Sunnah, which have exceeded the boundaries of the Sharee'ah legislated for refutations, then this is firstly should not to be attributed to the scholars in general, nor should be taken as a proof that we should remain silent from clarifying the truth of a matter, or cease refuting those who have differed with the evidences of Islaam.

This is the main point that I wished to warn against, and ❖ I only desire reform so far as I am able, to the best of my power. And my guidance cannot come except from Allaah, in Him I trust and unto Him I repent. ❖-(Surah Hud: 88) Peace and salutations be upon our Prophet Muhammad, upon his household, and his Companions."[10]

7. It is an avoidance of the sin of concealing knowledge.

The guiding leading scholar Sheikh 'Abdul-'Azeez Ibn 'Abdullah Ibn Baaz, may Allaah have mercy upon him, said,

"...After this it is upon the student of knowledge to be diligent in not concealing anything from the knowledge that he has learned. That he be diligent in explaining the truth, and refuting those who oppose what is known from the religion of Islaam, without him becoming lax in this or withdrawing himself and turning away from it. He should always be distinguished in this area of activity according to the limits of his capacity. Such that when the opponents of

[10] Source: al-Jazeerah magazine: Issue 11672, Yawn al-Ahad, Rajab 27, 1425

the truth come forward, resembling the people of the truth yet attacking them, he steps forward and excels in refuting them through writing, spoken statements, and in other ways.

He is not lax in this, saying 'This matter is for someone else'. Rather he should say, 'I will undertake it, I will undertake it'. And if there are others who are leading scholars who it is feared may have allowed an issue to pass them by, then he should be distinguished in standing forth to present it, not withdrawing from dealing with the matter. Indeed he should be distinguished by acting at the proper time in order to bring victory to the truth.

He should refute those who stand as opponents to the religion of Islaam through writing and other activities, such as by means of the media, through newspapers, through television, and through any means possible to accomplish this. Moreover, he must not conceal knowledge that he possesses; rather he must write and give sermons, speak and put forth refutations of the people of innovation in the religion as well as other than them from those who oppose some aspect of Islaam. He should undertake this with whatever Allaah has given him of strength, according to the degree of his knowledge, and what Allaah has made possible for him of various types of ability." [11]

8. It brings victory to Islaam despite the dislike of some people towards this practice.

As Sheikh Muqbil has mentioned:

"Therefore I say- no one knowingly turns away from understanding of this branch of knowledge except an individual who is ignorant, or an individual with a spiteful heart, or an individual who comes to know that he has himself been criticized. So he then has an aversion to

criticism and commendation in the religion due to the fact that he learns that he has been publicly criticized.

Yet Allaah rejects anything other than what brings victory to His religion and makes supreme His word, and brings forth the truth. Such that the people of the Sunnah have now given priority to criticism and commendation for the sake of the religion, And before it was as if some of them were sleeping, so Allaah facilitated for them those people those who would awaken them. As before some of them didn't used to speak extensively in matters of commendation and criticism- as if this was something specific to the period of Imaam al-Bukhaaree and Muslim..." [12]

It is left to the reader, after reading the words of the se people of knowledge brought forth in this small work, to consider and then humbly accept or falsely reject the evidences about refutations in general and attributing individuals to that which they themselves call to specifically. These scholars words indicate the necessity and importance for the Muslim Ummah of continually clarifying false:

a. concepts,
b. beliefs,
c. statements,
d. actions, and
e. methodologies

which are attributed to the religion of Islaam, and why it is essential to indicate and identify those misguided Muslims who openly hold and claim that they bring forth allegedly "good" changes, additions, and improvements to Islaam.

May Allaah grant us steadfastness upon His straight path, bless us to recognize the truth and adhere to it, and recognize falsehood and turn away from it.

[12] Advices & Clarifications: page 113

The Nakhlah Educational Series: Mission and Methodology (Pocket Edition)

Mission

The Purpose of the 'Nakhlah Educational Series' is to contribute to the present knowledge based efforts which enable Muslim individuals, families, and communities to understand and learn Islaam and then to develop within and truly live Islaam. Our commitment and goal is to contribute beneficial publications and works that:

Firstly, reflect the priority, message and methodology of all the prophets and messengers sent to humanity, meaning that single revealed message which embodies the very purpose of life, and of human creation. As Allaah the Most High has said,

❦ *We sent a Messenger to every nation ordering them that they should worship Allaah alone, obey Him and make their worship purely for Him, and that they should avoid everything worshipped besides Allaah. So from them there were those whom Allaah guided to His religion, and there were those who were unbelievers for whom misguidance was ordained. So travel through the land and see the destruction that befell those who denied the Messengers and disbelieved.*❦–(Surah an-Nahl: 36)

Two Essential Foundations

Secondly, building upon the above foundation, our commitment is to contributing publications and works which reflect the inherited message and methodology of the acknowledged scholars of the many various branches of Sharee'ah knowledge who stood upon the straight path of preserved guidance in every century and time since the time of our Messenger, may Allaah's praise and salutations be upon him. These people of knowledge, who are the inheritors of the Final Messenger, have always adhered closely to the two revealed sources of guidance: the Book of Allaah and the Sunnah of the Messenger of Allaah- may Allaah's praise and salutations be upon him, upon the united consensus, standing with the body of guided Muslims in every century - preserving and transmitting the true religion generation after generation. Indeed the Messenger of Allaah, may Allaah's praise and salutations be upon him, informed us that, *{ A group of people amongst my Ummah will remain obedient to Allaah's orders. They will not be harmed by those who leave them nor by those who oppose them, until Allaah's command for the Last Day comes upon them while they remain on the right path. }* (Authentically narrated in Saheeh al-Bukhaaree).

The guiding scholar Sheikh Zayd al-Madkhalee, may Allaah protect him, stated in his writing, 'The Well Established Principles of the Way of the First Generations of Muslims: It's Enduring & Excellent Distinct Characteristics' that,

"From among these principles and characteristics is that the methodology of tasfeeyah -or clarification, and tarbeeyah -or education and cultivation- is clearly affirmed and established as a true way coming from the first three generations of Islaam, and is something well known to the people of true merit from among them, as is concluded by considering all the related evidence. What is intended by tasfeeyah, when referring to it generally, is clarifying that which is the truth from that which is falsehood, what is goodness from that which is harmful and corrupt, and when referring to its specific meanings it is distinguishing the noble Sunnah of the Prophet and the people of the Sunnah from those innovated matters brought into the religion and the people who are supporters of such innovations.

As for what is intended by tarbeeyah, it is calling all of the creation to take on the manners and embrace the excellent character invited to by that guidance revealed to them by their

Lord through His worshiper and Messenger Muhammad, may Allaah's praise and salutations be upon him; so that they might have good character, manners, and behavior. As without this they cannot have a good life, nor can they put right their present condition or their final destination. And we seek refuge in Allaah from the evil of not being able to achieve that rectification."

Thus the methodology of the people of standing upon the Prophet's Sunnah, and proceeding upon the 'way of the believers' in every century is reflected in a focus and concern with these two essential matters: tasfeeyah or clarification of what is original, revealed message from the Lord of all the worlds, and tarbeeyah or education and raising of ourselves, our families, and our communities, and our lands upon what has been distinguished to be that true message and path.

Methodology:

The Roles of the Scholars & General Muslims In Raising the New Generation

The priority and focus of the 'Nakhlah Educational Series' is reflected within in the following statements of Sheikh al-Albaanee, may Allaah have mercy upon him:

"As for the other obligation, then I intend by this the education of the young generation upon Islaam purified from all of those impurities we have mentioned, giving them a correct Islamic education from their very earliest years, without any influence of a foreign, disbelieving education."

(Silsilat al-Hadeeth ad-Da'eefah, Introduction page 2.)

"...And since the Messenger of Allaah, may Allaah's praise and salutations be upon him, has indicated that the only cure to remove this state of humiliation that we find ourselves entrenched within, is truly returning back to the religion. Then it is clearly

obligatory upon us - through the people of knowledge- to correctly and properly understand the religion in a way that conforms to the sources of the Book of Allaah and the Sunnah, and that we educate and raise a new virtuous, righteous generation upon this."

(Clarification and Cultivation and the Need of the Muslims for Them)

It is essential in discussing our perspective upon this obligation of raising the new generation of Muslims, that we highlight and bring attention to a required pillar of these efforts as indicated by Sheikh al-Albaanee, may Allaah have mercy upon him, and others- in the golden words, *"through the people of knowledge"*. Since something we commonly experience today is that many people have various incorrect understandings of the role that the scholars should have in the life of a Muslim, failing to understand the way in which they fulfill their position as the inheritors of the Messenger of Allaah, may Allaah's praise and salutations be upon him, and stand as those who preserve and enable us to practice the guidance of Islaam.   Similarly the guiding scholar Sheikh 'Abdul-'Azeez Ibn Baaz, may Allaah have mercy upon him, also emphasized this same overall responsibility:

*"...It is also upon a Muslim that he struggles diligently in that which will place his worldly affairs in a good state, just as he must also strive in the correcting of his religious affairs and the affairs of his own family. As the people of his household have a significant right over him that he strive diligently in rectifying their affair and guiding them towards goodness, due to the statement of Allaah, the Most Exalted, ◊ **Oh you who believe! Save yourselves and your families Hellfire whose fuel is men and stones** ◊ -(Surah at-Tahreem: 6)*

So it is upon you to strive to correct the affairs of the members of your family. This includes your wife, your children- both male and female- and such as your own brothers. This concerns all of the people in your family, meaning you should strive to teach them the religion, guiding and directing them, and warning them from those matters Allaah has prohibited for us. Because you are the one who is responsible for them as shown in the statement of the Prophet, may Allaah's praise and salutations be upon him, *{ Every one of you is a guardian, and responsible for what is in his custody. The ruler is a guardian of his subjects and responsible for them; a husband is a guardian of his family and is responsible for it; a lady is a guardian of her husband's house and is responsible for it, and a servant is a guardian of his master's property and is responsible for it....}* Then the Messenger of Allaah, may Allaah's praise and salutations be upon him, continued to say, *{...so all of you are guardians and are responsible for those under your authority.}* (Authentically narrated in Saheeh al-Bukhaaree & Muslim)

It is upon us to strive diligently in correcting the affairs of the members of our families, from the aspect of purifying their sincerity of intention for Allaah's sake alone in all of their deeds, and ensuring that they truthfully believe in and follow the Messenger of Allaah, may Allaah's praise and salutations be upon him, their fulfilling the prayer and the other obligations which Allaah the Most Exalted has commanded for us, as well as from the direction of distancing them from everything which Allaah has prohibited.

It is upon every single man and women to give advice to their families about the fulfillment of what is obligatory upon them. Certainly, it is upon the woman as well as upon the man to perform this. In this way our homes become corrected and rectified in regard to the most important and essential matters. Allaah said to His Prophet, may Allaah's praise and salutations be upon him, ◈ *And enjoin the ritual prayers on your family...* ◈ (Surah Taha: 132) Similarly, Allaah the Most Exalted said to

His prophet Ismaa'aeel, ⟨ **And mention in the Book, Ismaa'aeel. Verily, he was true to what he promised, and he was a Messenger, and a Prophet. And he used to enjoin on his family and his people the ritual prayers and the obligatory charity, and his Lord was pleased with him.** ⟩ *-(Surah Maryam: 54-55)*

As such, it is only proper that we model ourselves after the prophets and the best of people, and be concerned with the state of the members of our households. Do not be neglectful of them, oh worshipper of Allaah! Regardless of whether it is concerning your wife, your mother, father, grandfather, grandmother, your brothers, or your children; it is upon you to strive diligently in correcting their state and condition..."

(Collection of Various Rulings and Statements- Sheikh 'Abdul-'Azeez Ibn 'Abdullah Ibn Baaz, Vol. 6, page 47)

Content & Structure:

We hope to contribute works which enable every striving Muslim who acknowledges the proper position of the scholars, to fulfill the recognized duty and obligation which lays upon each one of us to bring the light of Islaam into our own lives as individuals as well as into our homes and among our families. Towards this goal we are committed to developing educational publications and comprehensive educational curriculums -through cooperation with and based upon the works of the scholars of Islaam and the students of knowledge. Works which, with the assistance of Allaah, the Most High, we can utilize to educate and instruct ourselves, our families and our communities upon Islaam in both principle and practice. The publications and works of the Nakhlah Educational Series are divided into the following categories:

Basic: Ages 4- 6

Elementary: Ages 6-11

Secondary: Ages 11-14

High School: Ages 14- Young Adult

General: Young Adult –Adult

Supplementary: All Ages

Publications and works within these stated levels will, with the permission of Allaah, encompass different beneficial areas and subjects, and will be offered in every permissible form of media and medium. As certainly, as the guiding scholar Sheikh Saaleh Fauzaan al-Fauzaan, may Allaah preserve him, has stated,

"Beneficial knowledge is itself divided into two categories. Firstly is that knowledge which is tremendous in its benefit, as it benefits in this world and continues to benefit in the Hereafter. This is religious Sharee'ah knowledge. And secondly, that which is limited and restricted to matters related to the life of this world, such as learning the processes of manufacturing various goods. This is a category of knowledge related specifically to worldly affairs.

…As for the learning of worldly knowledge, such as knowledge of manufacturing, then it is legislated upon us collectively to learn whatever the Muslims have a need for. Yet If they do not have a need for this knowledge, then learning it is a neutral matter upon the condition that it does not compete with or displace any areas of Sharee'ah knowledge…"

("Explanations of the Mistakes of Some Writers"', Pages 10-12)

We ask Allaah, the most High to bless us with success in contributing to the many efforts of our Muslim brothers and sisters committed to raising themselves as individuals and the next generation of our children upon that Islaam which Allaah has perfected and chosen for us, and which He has enabled the guided Muslims to proceed upon in each and every century. We ask him to forgive us, and forgive the Muslim men and the Muslim women, and to guide all the believers to everything He loves and is pleased with. The success is from Allaah, The Most High The Most Exalted, alone and all praise is due to Him.

Abu Sukhailah Khalil Ibn-Abelahyi
Taalib al-Ilm Educational Resources

BOOK PUBLICATION PREVIEW:

Al-Waajibaat:
The Obligatory Matters

What it is Decreed that Every Male and Female Muslim Must Have Knowledge Of -from the statements of Sheikh al-Islaam Muhammad ibn 'Abdul-Wahaab

(A Step By Step Course on The Fundamental Beliefs of Islaam- with Lesson Questions, Quizzes, & Exams)

Collected and Arranged by
Umm Mujaahid Khadijah Bint Lacina
al-Amreekiyyah

[Available: **Now - Self Study/ Teachers Edition**
price: (Soft cover) **$20** (Hard cover) **$27**
Directed Study Edition price: **$17.50** -
Exercise Workbook price: **$10** ¦ eBook **$9.99**]

SCAN WITH SMARTPHONE

PRINT

FOR MORE INFORMATION

SCAN WITH SMARTPHONE

EBOOK

FOR MORE INFORMATION

BOOK PUBLICATION PREVIEW:

Statements of the Guiding Scholars of Our Age Regarding Books & their Advice to the Beginner Seeker of Knowledge

with Selections from the Following Scholars:
Sheikh 'Abdul-'Azeez ibn 'Abdullah ibn Baaz -Sheikh Muhammad ibn Saaleh al-'Utheimein - Sheikh Muhammad Naasiruddeen al-Albaanee - Sheikh Muqbil ibn Haadee al-Waada'ee - Sheikh 'Abdur-Rahman ibn Naaser as-Sa'adee - Sheikh Muhammad 'Amaan al-Jaamee - Sheikh Muhammad al-Ameen as-Shanqeetee - Sheikh Ahmad ibn Yahya an-Najmee & Sheikh Saaleh al-Fauzaan ibn 'Abdullah al-Fauzaan - Sheikh Saaleh ibn 'Abdul-'Azeez Aal-Sheikh - Sheikh Muhammad ibn 'Abdul-Wahhab al-Wasaabee -Permanent Committee to Scholastic Research & Issuing Of Islamic Rulings

With an introduction by: Sheikh Muhammad Ibn 'Abdullah al-Imaam
Collected and Translated by Abu Sukhailah Khalil Ibn-Abelahyi al-Amreekee

[Available: **Now** ¦ pages: 370+ ¦ price: (S) **$25**

(H) **$32** ¦ eBook **$9.99**]

SCAN WITH SMARTPHONE

PRINT

FOR MORE INFORMATION

SCAN WITH SMARTPHONE

EBOOK

FOR MORE INFORMATION

BOOK PUBLICATION PREVIEW:

Thalaathatu al-Usool: The Three Fundamental Principles

A Step by Step Educational Course on Islaam
Based upon Commentaries of 'Thalaathatu al-Usool'
of Sheikh Muhammad ibn 'Abdul Wahaab
(may Allaah have mercy upon him)

*Collected and Arranged by Umm Mujaahid
Khadijah Bint Lacina al-Amreekiyyah*

Description:

*A complete course for the Believing men and women
who want to learn their religion from the ground
up, building a firm foundation upon which to base
their actions. This is the* **second** *in our* **Foundation
Series** *on Islamic beliefs and making them a reality
in your life, which began with* **"al-Waajibaat: The
Obligatory Matters"**.

[Available: **Now Self Study/ Teachers Edition** ¦
price: (Soft cover) **$22.50** (Hard cover) **$29.50**
Directed Study Edition price: (S) **$17.50** -
Exercise Workbook price: (S) **$10** ¦ eBook **$9.99**]

SCAN WITH SMARTPHONE

PRINT

FOR MORE INFORMATION

SCAN WITH SMARTPHONE

EBOOK

FOR MORE INFORMATION

BOOK PUBLICATION PREVIEW:

My Hijaab, My Path

A Comprehensive Knowledge Based Compilation on Muslim Women's Role & Dress

Collected and Translated by
Umm Mujaahid Khadijah Bint Lacina
al-Amreekiyyah

[Available: **Now** ¦ pages: **190+** ¦ price: (S) **$17.50**
(H) **$25** ¦ eBook **$9.99**

SCAN WITH SMARTPHONE

PRINT

FOR MORE INFORMATION

SCAN WITH SMARTPHONE

EBOOK

FOR MORE INFORMATION

BOOK PUBLICATION PREVIEW:

Fasting from Alif to Yaa:

A Day by Day Guide to Making the Most of Ramadhaan

-Contains additional points of benefit to teach one how to live Islaam as a way of life
-Plus, stories of the Prophets and Messengers including activities for the whole family to enjoy and benefit from for each day of Ramadhaan. Some of the Prophets and Messengers covered include Aadam, Ibraaheem, Lut, Yusuf, Sulaymaan, Shu'ayb, Moosa, Zakariyyah, Muhammad, and more! -Recipes for foods enjoyed by Muslims around the world

By Umm Mujaahid Khadijah Bint Lacina al-Amreekiyyah as-Salafiyyah With Abu Hamzah Hudhaifah Ibn Khalil and Umm Usaamah Sukhailah Bint Khalil

[Available: **1433** -pages: 250+ ¦ price: (S) **$20** (H) **$27** ¦ eBook **$9.99**

BOOK PUBLICATION PREVIEW:

Whispers of Paradise (1): A Muslim Woman's Life Journal

An Islamic Daily Journal Which Encourages Reflection & Rectification

Collected and Edited by Taalib al-Ilm Educational Resources Development Staff

[Available: **Now** ¦ price: (Hard cover) **$32**]

[Elegantly designed edition is for the year 1434 / 2013]

12 Monthly calendar pages with beneficial quotations from Ibn Qayyim
Daily journal page based upon Islamic calendar (with corresponding C.E. dates)

SCAN WITH SMARTPHONE

FOR MORE INFORMATION

www.ingramcontent.com/pod-product-compliance
Lightning Source LLC
Chambersburg PA
CBHW030108070426
42448CB00036B/479